Nonparametric Projections of Forest and Rangeland Condition Indicators

JOHN HOF, CURTIS FLATHER, TONY BALTIC, AND RUDY KING

*A Technical Document Supporting
the USDA Forest Service 2005 Update of the RPA Assessment*

U.S. DEPARTMENT OF AGRICULTURE FOREST SERVICE

Hof, John; Flather, Curtis; Baltic, Tony; King, Rudy. 2006. **Nonparametric projections of forest and rangeland condition indicators: A technical document supporting the 2005 USDA Forest Service RPA Assessment Update.** Gen. Tech. Rep. RMRS-GTR-166. Fort Collins, CO: U.S. Department of Agriculture, Forest Service, Rocky Mountain Research Station. 39 p.

Abstract

The 2005 Forest and Rangeland Condition Indicator Model is a set of classification trees for forest and rangeland condition indicators at the national scale. This report documents the development of the database and the nonparametric statistical estimation for this analytical structure, with emphasis on three special characteristics of condition indicator production processes: (1) the inability of humans to completely control ecological systems; (2) the lack of a theoretical basis for specific relational functional forms, suggesting the need for a highly flexible model structure; and (3) the broad-scale spatial nature of the problem (and data). The resolution of data deficiencies is also examined. Finally, the model projections themselves are presented and discussed using national-scale maps.

Keywords: Resource interactions, land management planning, classification trees, modeling, environmental outputs

Authors

John Hof is a Research Forester (retired), Rocky Mountain Research Station, USDA Forest Service, Fort Collins, CO.

Curtis Flather is a Research Wildlife Biologist, Rocky Mountain Research Station, USDA Forest Service, Fort Collins, CO.

Tony Baltic is an Operations Research Analyst, Rocky Mountain Research Station, USDA Forest Service, Fort Collins, CO.

Rudy King is Station Statistician, Rocky Mountain Research Station, USDA Forest Service, Fort Collins, CO.

Nonparametric Projections of Forest and Rangeland Condition Indicators: A Technical Document Supporting the 2005 USDA Forest Service RPA Assessment Update

John Hof, Curtis Flather, Tony Baltic, and Rudy King

Contents

Background

The Forest and Rangeland Renewable Resources Planning Act of 1974 (RPA) as amended by the National Forest Management Act of 1976 (NFMA) and the six national renewable resource assessments that have been completed as mandated by that legislation have all emphasized the importance of quantitative information on renewable resource interactions. The interactions analysis for the 1989 RPA Assessment (Hof and Baltic 1988) focused on the National Forest System lands. That report analyzed the capability of the National Forest System to maintain a constant share of total national resource production, as indicated by the demand (consumption) projections developed for individual resources in other recent assessment analyses and the impacts on costs and environmental conditions. The analysis was not completely successful in determining the environmental impacts of increasing output levels, but it did indicate previously unrecognized limits to the production capabilities of the National Forest System. These results were used in the development of the Recommended 1990 RPA Program (USDA Forest Service 1990). In the "Implications" chapter, the Program also emphasized the critical importance of interactions research:

> Without improved information [about resource interactions], there could be misjudgments about the resource output capability of the Nation's forests and rangelands. This could
>
> - Lead to errors in management decisions that could stress the resource base or, conversely, underutilize the resource capability.
>
> - Misdirect public and private programs that target just one renewable resource, without giving adequate attention to effects on other resources.

Since that assessment and program development, the Forest Service has undergone a significant change in the way it considers and manages natural resources. The 1989 interactions analysis focused on harvestable resource outputs and the 1990 Program endorsed this approach to interactions analyses when it stated that the objective of research in resource interactions "is to determine which management systems and practices are most suitable for the production and use of natural resources." In 1992, however, the Forest Service officially committed to using an approach to management called "ecosystem management" defined as "an ecological approach to achieve the multiple-use management of the National Forests and Grasslands by blending the needs of people and environmental values in such a way that the National Forests and Grasslands represent diverse, healthy, productive, and sustainable ecosystems" (Robertson 1992). The subsequent 1993 RPA Assessment Update (USDA Forest Service 1994) stated in the section on "Ecosystems Management and Resource Interactions," that "an emphasis on ecosystem management may change the nature of production possibilities and feasibilities." This section concluded that future resource interactions analyses needed to involve "assessments of [ecosystem] function, process, and condition." Both the 1993 Update and the Draft 1995 RPA Program (USDA Forest Service 1995) continued to emphasize the importance of resource interactions research, but within this new context.

Based on this new direction for management and research, the 2000 resource interactions model and supporting database (Hof and others 1999a, b) was oriented toward analysis of the interactions between resource use and condition indicators, as opposed to the emphasis on production possibilities and feasibilities in the 1989 interactions analysis. The focus on condition indicators is a direct result of a shift in natural resource management that is now focusing on long-term sustainability of ecosystems as the measure of responsible stewardship (Nobel and Dirzo 1997; Heinz Center 2002). This shift is attributable to a growing recognition that the human economy is very much dependent upon goods and services derived directly from ecosystems (Dailey 1997) and that intensive use of natural resources may be stressing ecosystems to a point where their ability to provide these benefits is compromised (Vitousek and others 1997; Loreau and others 2001). The 2000 analysis used econometric methods to project "hotspots" of stress as suggested by a set of forest and rangeland condition indicators. Now, for the 2005 Update of the 2000 Assessment, a new model has been built that has an improved set of indicators, a more tenable set of driving variable projections, and a more flexible, nonparametric methodology. Although the indicators of forest and rangeland condition chosen were limited by data availability, they were chosen to reflect (as much as possible) the scope and intent of ongoing efforts to define appropriate sets of ecosystem condition indicators (Rapport and others 1985; Coulombe 1995; National Research Council 2000). This report describes the rationale and structure of this new model, the development of its supporting database, the implementation of the model in projecting hotspots for resource condition indicators, and the results of our analysis as displayed with national-level maps.

Structure of the Model____

The purpose of this analysis is to identify broad-scale (national) relationships between natural characteristics, land use/land cover/land ownership variables, human population, and indicators of the forest and rangeland condition. Many studies have quantified these types of relationships at the local scale (see Hof and Baltic [1988] for a survey). Far less is known about these relationships at the national scale, other than the econometric results of our previous study (Hof and others 1998). This study does not analyze biological processes or capture detailed impacts. Rather, its intent is to analyze coarse effects at a very broad spatial scale. This study certainly misses many fine-scale relationships, but it may capture broad-scale effects that are missed with a tightly focused view. We are, so to speak, trying to see the forest, not the trees. We begin with a brief discussion of the theory behind this analysis and then focus on the suggested empirics.

The production processes for the indicators of forest and rangeland condition are obviously different from those for traditional economic outputs. The ecosystems that "produce" environmental outputs on forests and rangelands are far more complex and far less controllable by human management than a traditional economic production unit such as a factory or a farm. In addition, the production unit for forest and rangeland ecosystems covers very large landscapes rather than the spatially limited traditional economic production units. Thus, in this paper, we will focus on three special characteristics of the environmental output production process: (1) the inability of humans to completely control ecological systems; (2) the lack of a theoretical basis for specific relational functional forms, suggesting the need for a highly flexible model structure; and (3) the broad-scale spatial nature of the problem (and data). Each of these will be discussed in more detail before proceeding.

Ecosystem Independence

First, we define three vectors of variables: $\tilde{X}$ is a vector of inputs that include human-generated inputs embodied in management actions as well as "natural" inputs such as climate and landscape characteristics; $\tilde{Y}$ is a vector of harvested outputs such as timber, livestock grazing, recreation use, and mining activity; and $\tilde{Z}$ is a vector of forest and rangeland condition indicators. The traditional economic analysis would treat the $\tilde{Y}$ vector as the outputs, produced from the $\tilde{X}$ vector, with the $\tilde{Z}$ vector left largely unaccounted for. Our focus here is the $\tilde{Z}$ vector, so we will treat it as the output vector with the $\tilde{X}$ and $\tilde{Y}$ vectors as inputs. It might be more appealing in this context to regard the $\tilde{Y}$ vector as harvest-related management intensity variables that are inputs (positive or negative) to the production of the condition indicators.

The textbook treatment of joint production would use an implicit-form production function as:

$$0 = f\left(\tilde{X}, \tilde{Y}, \tilde{Z}\right) \qquad (1)$$

to relate these three variable vectors. Mittelhammer and others (1981) show, however, that this approach is quite limiting because it does not allow any of the variables (and $\tilde{Z}$ in our case) to be unrelated. In a traditional economic production unit, we expect to be able to fix inputs and then define a locus of output combinations—the product transformation curve. Because our outputs are the $\tilde{Z}$ forest and rangeland condition indicators, this expectation may not be appropriate. In ecological systems theory, management actions are viewed as altering the structure and function of the ecosystem, which then results in a particular system response (see Barrett and others 1976; Hall and Day 1977; Allen and Hoekstra 1992). Viewed deterministically, any combination of $\tilde{X}$ and $\tilde{Y}$ is associated with a particular set of environmental outputs $\tilde{Z}$, and the product transformation curve would be a single point. For example, once a certain fire suppression and harvesting schedule is applied, a set of environmental outputs such as sedimentation and wildlife habitat are determined by the resulting ecosystem structure and function. This would suggest that an appropriate production structure should have the property that:

$$\partial Z_i / \partial Z_j = 0 \qquad i \neq j \qquad (2)$$

with all $\tilde{X}$ and $\tilde{Y}$ held constant. Mittelhammer and others show that such a property is not obtainable with (1). A production structure that has this property would be:

$$Z_i = g_i\left(\tilde{X}, \tilde{Y}\right) \forall i. \qquad (3)$$

Note that (3) is not a simultaneous system, but is potentially a set of seemingly unrelated regressions. Equation (3) is still a joint production structure, because the $\tilde{Z}$ simultaneously utilize the $\tilde{X}$ and $\tilde{Y}$ inputs. If the $\tilde{X}$ and $\tilde{Y}$ vectors are fixed, however, only a single $\tilde{Z}$ results, reflecting the autonomy of the ecosystem, as desired. In a complex ecosystem, interactions between any of the $\tilde{X}$ and $\tilde{Y}$ variables in affecting the $\tilde{Z}$ variables are potentially important, suggesting the flexible, interactive approach referred to as "Classification Trees" (discussed next).

Classification Tree Structure

The ultimate purpose of this study is to project "hotspots" of environmental stress. We will use indicators of forest and rangeland condition stress (environmental outputs) to accomplish this purpose, and the current hotspots for each indicator will be defined as the areas in the country with the highest 10 percent of the values for that indicator. When we project these hotspots, this definition will be retained—we will project areas that, in the future, would be considered hotspots by our current standard just defined. Thus, analytically, we have a classification problem and we need a flexible classification tool that can be used for projection purposes. Let us look at the need for flexibility a bit closer.

The production functions in (3) are written in closed form for the purposes of discussion, but it is actually quite difficult to determine what sort of specific functional form would be theoretically tenable for such a relationship. In Hof and others (1999a, b), we used a translog functional form to be as flexible as possible in a (parametric) econometric estimation. However, the relationships between variables and environmental outputs may be strongly nonlinear and involve complex interaction terms that remain undetectable by traditional statistical modeling approaches (De' ath and Fabricius 2000). An alternative modeling approach that can represent complex variable interactions and is robust to violation of assumptions that typically constrain parametric modeling techniques is called "classification and regression trees" (CART; see Breiman and others 1984). A CART model can be built for either a categorical (generating a classification tree) or continuous (generating a regression tree) response variable. Because our interest lies in projecting whether a given geographic unit qualifies as a hotspot of environmental stress (a categorical response), we will generate a set of classification trees.

A classification tree amounts to a set of binary differentiations ("splits"), each based on a threshold value of a particular explanatory variable. The explanatory variable and its associated threshold value (split point) are selected in the CART algorithm so as to minimize a "misclassification function." At each split observations are partitioned into two groups, with the set of observations in each partition being more homogeneous with respect to membership in the response variable's categorical classes than the set of observations prior to the split. The CART classification algorithm continues to construct additional splitting rules until all observations are assigned to class categories in a way that minimizes misclassification. This initial classification tree is then "pruned" in a search for the simplest tree without significantly eroding classification accuracy (Breiman and others 1984:59-81). The CART software uses "10-fold" cross-validation of the tree estimation process to compute an unbiased estimate of misclassification rate (Steinberg and Colla 2000). In this fashion CART essentially specifies a dichotomous key that is used to assign new observations to the response variable categories. Flexibility is achieved because no pre-specifications on the structure or content of the trees are necessary.

In this paper, the coterminous United States is divided into a grid of uniform-sized cells, which we call "analysis grid cells." The objective is to classify all analysis grid cells as a "hotspot" or a "non-hotspot" with regard to each of a set of indicators. The discussion above suggests that each indicator should be analyzed separately, so a classification tree will be estimated for each indicator. Figure 1 presents a very simple example. Each node in the inverted tree represents the separation of analysis grid cells into two groups. For example, the first node separates the cells into two groups depending on each cell's value for the variable "Agr." Those cells that have more than 85 percent of their land in agricultural land use are then further split according to the variable Urb reflecting the percent of the cell in urban land. The cells that have less than 85 percent of their land in agricultural land use are further split according to their density of human population (pop/acre). The binary splits continue until all of the cells are classified into sets that are labeled as either "hotspot" or "non-hotspot." These final sets are referred to as terminal nodes and together they represent a mutually exclusive and exhaustive partitioning of all analysis grid cells. Once a classification tree has been constructed, projections of hotspot and non-hotspot sets can be obtained by substituting the projected values of the explanatory variables associated with each analysis grid cell and allowing the tree to re-classify these "new" cells.

Spatial considerations are critical both in the process of estimating classification trees and in the process of using them for projection purposes. These spatial factors are discussed next.

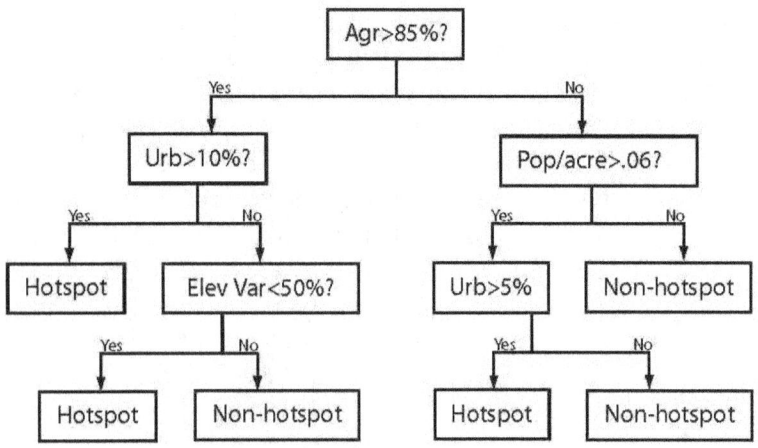

Figure 1. An Example Classification Tree.

Spatial Considerations

Because the problem defined for this paper has a large spatial extent and because the process of producing environmental outputs takes place over very large landscapes, the estimation of the desired functions requires consideration of spatial issues that are not normally a concern in traditional economic models of production. Our desired sampling scheme for environmental output production analyses would yield observations that: (1) provide a representative sample of all ecological systems in the study area; and (2) provide a reasonable representation of the system's boundary when aggregated by ecosystem. Unfortunately, broad-scale data are often not available on this basis. At our scale, data are available in many different formats, from micro data with many sample points to county-level numbers that are relatively reliable but are also highly aggregated. This was problematic since we needed to have our response and explanatory variables on a common spatial frame.

In Hof and others (1999a, b), we tested two approaches to this problem. The "COUNTY" approach simply aggregated all micro data into county averages and treated the county as the observation unit. This approach is typical in broad scale statistical modeling (see Cressie 1991:383), but differential county size results in inequitable sampling of landscapes across the coterminous United States. In our "GRID" approach, we started with the data in its most disaggregated (and nonhomogeneously defined) format, and then we used kriging (Robertson 2000) to spatially interpolate observations onto a uniform grid across the country (the reader is referred to Cressie [1991], Ripley [1981], and Haining [1990] for a detailed discussion of kriging and geostatistical techniques in general). This approximated the more equitable sampling scheme that would have been desirable in the first place. Using this intermediate step increases the possibility of information loss from smoothing or averaging in the interpolation process but creates a much more homogenous spatial density of observation units than counties.

The results of the test in Hof and others (1999a, b) suggested statistical advantages in the GRID approach, and it has two particular advantages in this study. First, in the classification tree method, goodness of fit is largely based on counts of misclassified observations. If the observations are of heterogeneous size then these goodness of fit measures are more difficult to interpret and are less reliable. Second, the interpretation of the classification tree and the definition of the hotspots projected with it are much more straightforward if the observations are of uniform size. We did experiment with the COUNTY approach in CART and found that the indicated performance was greatly superior with the GRID approach.

In Hof and others (1999a,b), we maintained approximately the same number of observations in the GRID approach as there were in the COUNTY approach, because we did not want to inflate the statistical hypothesis tests by artificially increasing sample size. In this case, however, the nonparametric model is not influenced by sample size, and we wanted to retain as much detail as possible (especially in the parts of the country with small counties). Thus, the analysis grid that we implemented contained 17,000 cells, which resulted in a cell size (21,376.5 meters square or 45,695.5 ha) that approximated the 5 percent quantile level of county sizes (only 5 percent of the counties in the coterminous United States are smaller than our cell size).

Database Development____

The theoretical production structure discussed above suggests that indicators of forest and rangeland condition should be related to measures (including surrogate measures) of land use, land ownership, climate variables, topography variables, human population levels, economic activity levels, and commodity harvest levels. For purposes of projecting hotspots, however, projections of these explanatory variables are needed, and geographically specific projections are only available for land use/land cover variables (Alig and others 2003) and for human population (Woods and Poole Economics, Inc. 2003). In addition, we assumed that climate, topography, and land ownership variables are constant during the projection period (to 2025). We limited the variables in the projection model to these, so as to maximize the explanatory power of the variables that we have projections for. Including explanatory variables that cannot be tenably projected has the potential to compromise the power of the explanatory variables that we do have projections for and also to create a scenario among the explanatory variable projections that is internally inconsistent. This points up the most critical weakness of projection models—the projection of the response variable is only as good as the projections of the explanatory variables that are available. Of course, the question remains: are these explanatory variables sufficient for the classification tree to be able to generate tenable hotspot projections? Basically, the hypothesis is that population, land ownership, and the land use/land cover variables capture the basic pattern of human activity and that the climate and topography variables capture the environmental context. Our CART estimations will provide a test of this hypothesis below. We should note that the available projections of the explanatory variables are defined on a county basis, so they needed to be translated onto our uniform grid by spatially interpolating (kriging) from county centroids to grid centroids.

The database includes 10 response variables representing forest and rangeland conditions. Based on the previous discussion, we included 21 explanatory variables including seven measures of human activity (including six land use/land cover types and human population), two variables that relate to federal/nonfederal ownership, a categorical variable to account for ecoregional differences, and 11 measures of climate and topographic variation. All of these were included in model estimation, and then the ownership, ecoregional strata, and climate and topographic variables were assumed constant in the projection of the hotspots.

All of these variables are defined, with sources, in Appendix A. Again, only the coterminous United States is included. Data were obtained from numerous sources in formats ranging from digital spatial databases to highly aggregated county data and micro data with many sample points. Most of the source databases included many variables and individual variables were often reported in multiple temporal and spatial dimensions. Thus, extraction was a significant undertaking. The digital data required geospatial analysis using a Geographic Information System (GIS) and other data had to be reformatted or otherwise processed and synthesized to be consistent with the data structure requirements of the analytical approach. This processing was not trivial because of the spatial scope of the analysis, the wide range of the variables of interest, and the sheer magnitude and complexity of many of the source databases. Data gaps were particularly problematic because the threshold for rejecting variables on the grounds of insufficient coverage is not clear. Interpolations and other estimations were necessary to ensure data completeness of the variables included. As indicated earlier, kriging was used to extrapolate micro level data to the grid structure and to interpolate county level data to the grid structure.

Standardization involved four kinds of processing. First, for county data, there were some data with observations for different parts of a given county that had to be averaged or apportioned to obtain a single county observation. Second, spatial standardization to a common land area (acres) was often required because counties and other spatial reporting areas (for example, watersheds) vary greatly in size. Third, temporal standardization was also necessary for data that varied over time (climate data for example). Fourth, much of the data had to be standardized to analysis grid cells in a GIS geospatial analysis involving the calculation of "zonal means" (where the analysis grid cells were defined as the zones).

Georeferencing, the geographic location of data, was another necessary processing step. An identifier was assigned as a unique variable for each data observation representing either a land area or specific point on the ground. For example, FIPS codes identify the county data and each observation in the grid data is identified by a geographic coordinate (point of latitude and longitude) for the cell centroid. These centroids represent the observation units in the grid model structure.

The sources and processing procedures are unique to each variable and, again, are summarized in Appendix A for each variable included in the analysis. All

Table 1. Goodness of fit statistics for classification trees.

Indicator	No. of terminal nodes	Test data % error			Learning data % error		
		False Non-hotspot	False Hotspot	Total	False Non-hotspot	False Hotspot	Total
EDG	97	14.29	13.42	13.51	5.24	11.96	11.29
PCH	70	13.47	10.25	10.57	5.88	9.47	9.11
EXT	75	4.47	2.45	2.65	0.12	1.90	1.72
MOR	101	7.71	3.73	4.13	0.70	2.74	2.54
GRO	78	7.20	6.13	6.24	0.91	5.37	4.92
STR	149	15.82	11.29	11.75	2.59	10.56	9.76
NTG	213	17.12	7.35	8.32	1.47	5.88	5.44
PHO	188	19.00	9.27	10.25	2.47	8.74	8.11
PHL	81	3.18	2.82	2.86	0.12	2.62	2.19
TRI	68	6.06	10.00	9.61	1.18	7.55	6.91

database files and documentation are stored at the Rocky Mountain Research Station, Fort Collins, Colorado.

Model Estimation and Results

Classification trees were estimated for each of the 10 forest and rangeland condition indicators using the procedures in Breiman and others (1984). These trees attempt to correctly classify the current hotspots from the database just described. Table 1 presents the basic measures of goodness of fit for this nonparametric estimation procedure. Overall, the results are fairly encouraging. The total classification errors in the estimation of the trees (the LEARNING data errors) are typically less than 10 percent, and the TEST data errors typically total less than 12 percent. The TEST data errors are based on a 10-fold cross-validation test, as mentioned earlier (see Breiman and others 1984; Steinberg and Colla 2000). In terms of model error, our main concern is the false hotspot errors, because of the possibility that they would influence the hotspot projections. In a later section, we will plot the false hotspot cells from the CART estimation and compare them to the actual current hotspots. Overall, there is typically a spatial association between the actual hotspots and the false hotspot errors. This suggests that when the classification trees make systematic errors, it is on the margin of the hotspot areas (which is what one might hope for).

The results in table 1 suggest that the variables included in the model (for projection purposes) do appear to be adequate to provide a fairly accurate classification of current hotspots with the CART algorithm. Thus, for our purposes here, we will tentatively accept the hypothesis that these explanatory variables adequately provide for a classification of analysis grid cells into hotspot and non-hotspot groups for the indicator variables included. Caveats regarding our projections based on this model will be emphasized in the Conclusion.

Projection of Explanatory Variables

Using the classification trees to project changes in forest and rangeland condition indicators over time required the projection of selected explanatory variables. FED and PAD were assumed to be constant because RPA assessments in the past have concluded that ownership patterns for forest and rangeland are expected to change little over the projection period (USDA Forest Service 1989). The climate and topography variables were assumed to be constant (recognizing that we are ignoring the possibility of global climate change within the projection time period). Projections to the year 2025 were developed for the land use/land cover and human population variables: RNG, CRO, FOR, DEV, PAS, CRP, and POP (described in Appendix A). Projections for the land use/cover variables were based on projections from Alig and others (2003). These projections were county-based and only applied to non-federal land. Land uses on federal land were assumed to be constant throughout the projection period based on the findings of recent RPA assessments of land use and land cover changes (USDA Forest Service 1989; 2001). County-level projections for population (POP) were obtained from Woods & Poole Economics, Inc.

(2003) an independent corporation that specializes in long-term county economic and demographic projections. All of the explanatory variable projections (that change) are mapped in Appendix B.

Projection of Forest and Rangeland Condition Indicators

The classification tree is used to project hotspots for each indicator by inserting the projected values of the explanatory variables and then reclassifying all cells accordingly, as previously discussed. For each indicator, we report three maps: (a) the current condition hotspots, (b) the false hotspot errors from the estimation of the CART model, and (c) the CART model hotspot projections for the year 2025. The false hotspot errors are areas where the CART model classified cells as current hotspots, but they are actually non-hotspots (these errors were tabulated in table 1). These errors may be pure model errors, or they could reflect areas that are "very nearly" hotspots.

The false hotspot error maps are important to consider when viewing the CART projections, because the projections inevitably include model error (and the only indication we have of those are the false hotspot errors for the current time period). It is impossible to determine if any false hotspot errors that appear in the projections occur because of pure model error or because they are currently trending toward being hotspots. An area that is erroneously predicted by CART to be a current hotspot might be correctly projected to be a future hotspot by the same model, and vice-versa. Such is the nature of statistical projection modeling. Clearly, the hotspots discussed should be regarded as candidates for further study—our analysis is suggestive, not definitive in projecting trends.

Individual Indicator Hotspot Projections

Edge (EDG)

As the amount of native habitat is reduced, there comes a point when the arrangement of that habitat becomes critically important to maintaining ecosystems (Saunders and others 1991; Muradian 2001). Edge effects are thought to be a predominant factor affecting the structure and function of ecological systems (Harrison and Bruna 1999). Although most of the empirical literature has focused on documenting edge effects at local scales, there is accumulating evidence that the influence of edges can be wide-ranging, affecting ecosystem properties over broad geographic regions (Laurance 2000).

Current condition hotspots for the amount of edge between native habitats and human-dominated land uses are generally scattered across the country, with some concentrations in the eastern half of the country (figure 2a). The false hotspot errors from the CART model (figure 2b) are also more concentrated in the east and do tend to be located on the fringes of the current hotspot concentrations. The CART model projects significant increases in the hotspot areas by 2025, with new hotspot areas being very much concentrated in the eastern half of the country (figure 2c).

Patch Size (PCH)

Another attribute of habitat arrangement that affects ecosystem structure and function is the size of patches on a landscape. One of the most obvious, and nearly ever-present, effects of habitat destruction is a reduction in average patch size (Bender and others 1998). Reductions in the average size of patches can compound the effects associated with a loss of habitat (Flather and Bevers 2002) stemming from a reduced capacity to support biological diversity, altered disturbance regimes, and subtle changes to microclimate (Saunders and others 1991).

Current concentrations of low average patch size for native habitats are fairly clustered in the upper Midwest and Great Lake states (figure 3a). Peninsular Florida, the Gulf coast, and the entire West also exhibit some smaller current condition hotspot areas. The false hotspot errors from the CART model (figure 3b) are quite scattered but still appear to be associated spatially with the current hotspots. The CART model projects increases in the PCH hotspots by 2025, located similarly to the current condition hotspots (figure 3c). The increases seem particularly noticeable in Florida, California, Arizona, New Mexico, and the Midwest from Texas north to North Dakota and east to Ohio.

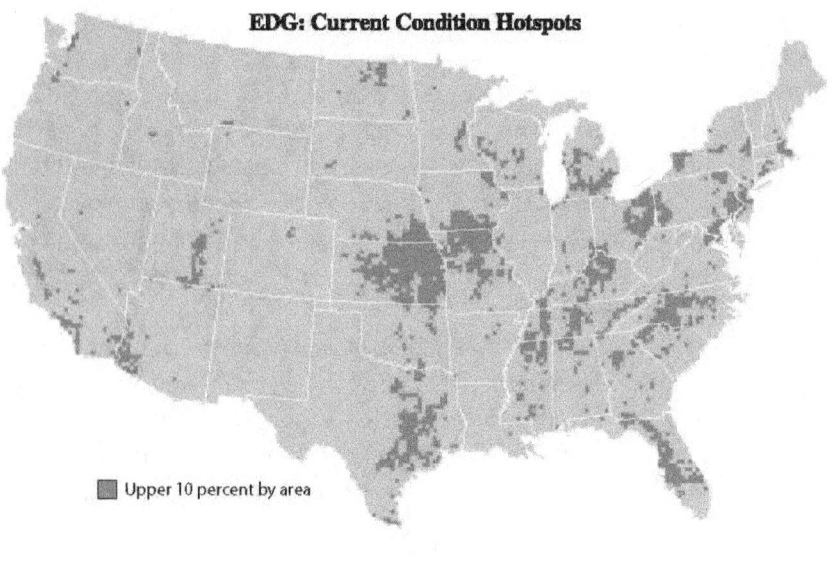

EDG: Current Condition Hotspots

■ Upper 10 percent by area

Figure 2. (a) Current Condition Hotspots, (b) False Hotspot Errors from
the CART Model, and (c) Projected
CART Model Hotspots to 2025
for EDG. The Current Condition
Hotspots are the grid cells with the
worst 10 percent of the EDG values
in the current data set, the False
Hotspot Errors are the grid cells
that the CART model incorrectly
classified as hotspots based on
the current values for the independent variables, and the Projected
Hotspots are the grid cells that the
CART model classified as hotspots
based on the projected values of the
independent variables.

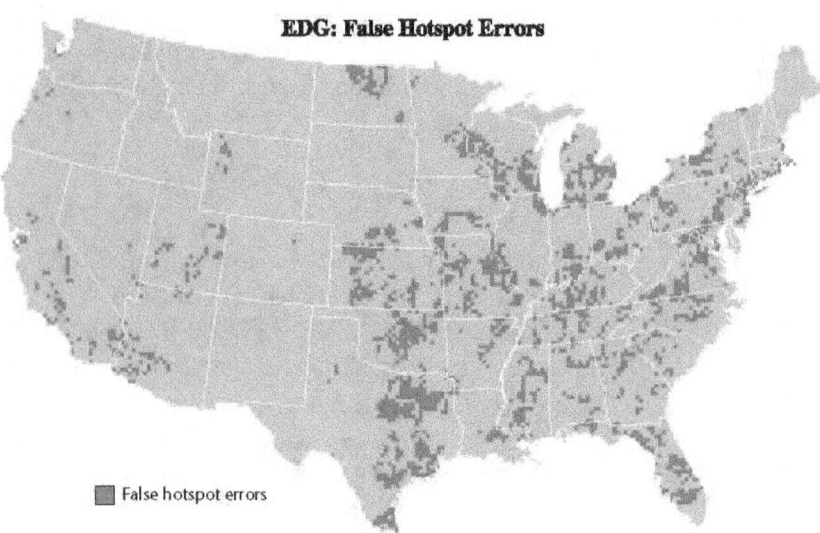

EDG: False Hotspot Errors

■ False hotspot errors

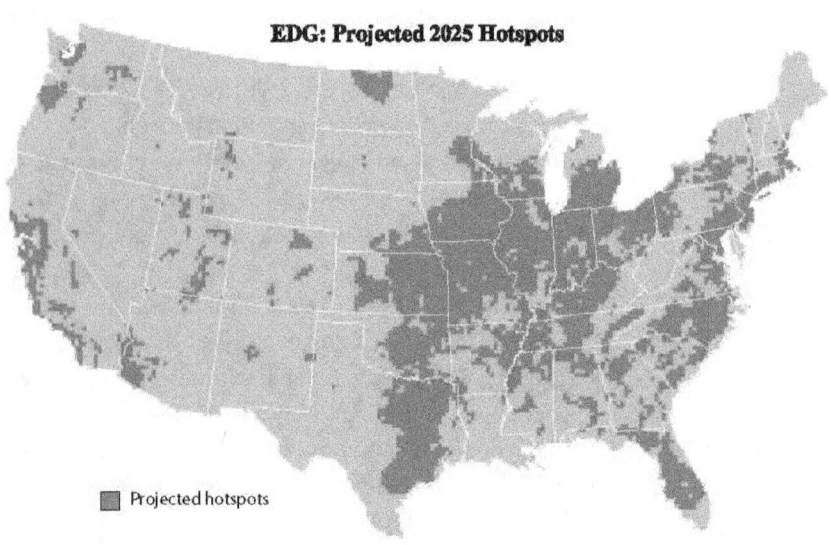

EDG: Projected 2025 Hotspots

■ Projected hotspots

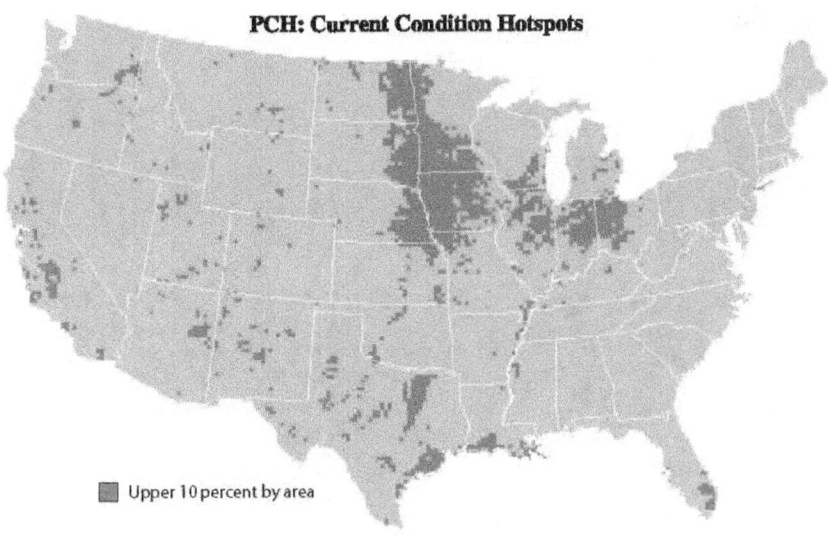

PCH: Current Condition Hotspots

☐ Upper 10 percent by area

PCH: False Hotspot Errors

☐ False hotspot errors

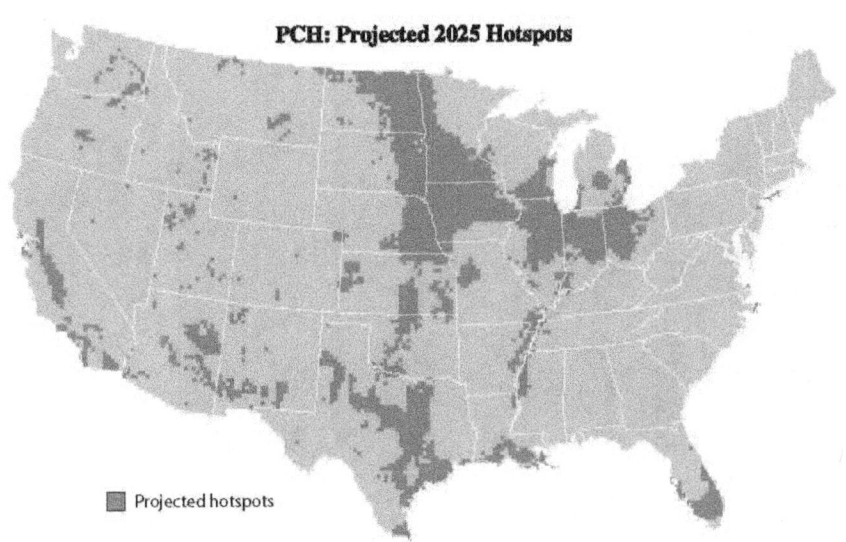

PCH: Projected 2025 Hotspots

☐ Projected hotspots

Figure 3. (a) Current Condition Hotspots, (b) False Hotspot Errors from the CART Model, and (c) Projected CART Model Hotspots to 2025 for PCH. The Current Condition Hotspots are the grid cells with the worst 10 percent of the PCH values in the current data set, the False Hotspot Errors are the grid cells that the CART model incorrectly classified as hotspots based on the current values for the independent variables, and the Projected Hotspots are the grid cells that the CART model classified as hotspots based on the projected values of the independent variables.

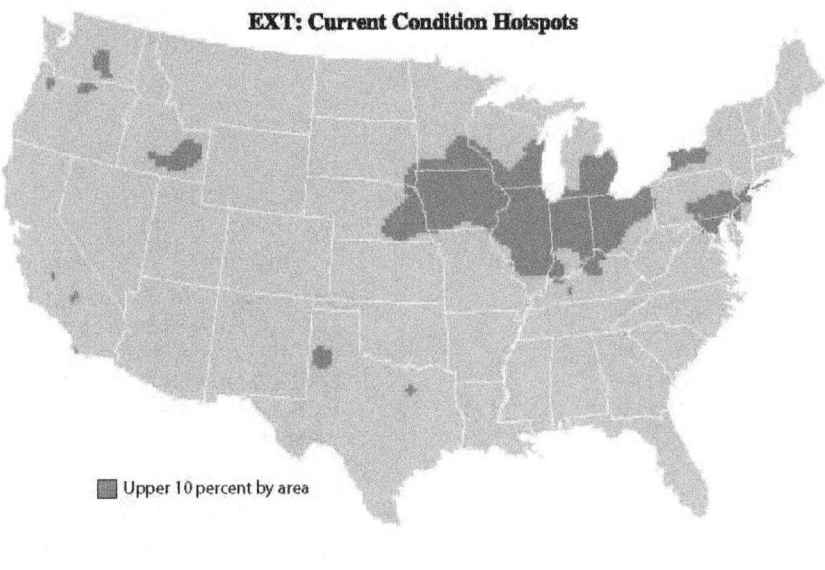

EXT: Current Condition Hotspots

Upper 10 percent by area

Figure 4. (a) Current Condition Hotspots, (b) False Hotspot Errors from the CART Model, and (c) Projected CART Model Hotspots to 2025 for EXT. The Current Condition Hotspots are the grid cells with the worst 10 percent of the EXT values in the current data set, the False Hotspot Errors are the grid cells that the CART model incorrectly classified as hotspots based on the current values for the independent variables, and the Projected Hotspots are the grid cells that the CART model classified as hotspots based on the projected values of the independent variables.

EXT: False Hotspot Errors

False hotspot errors

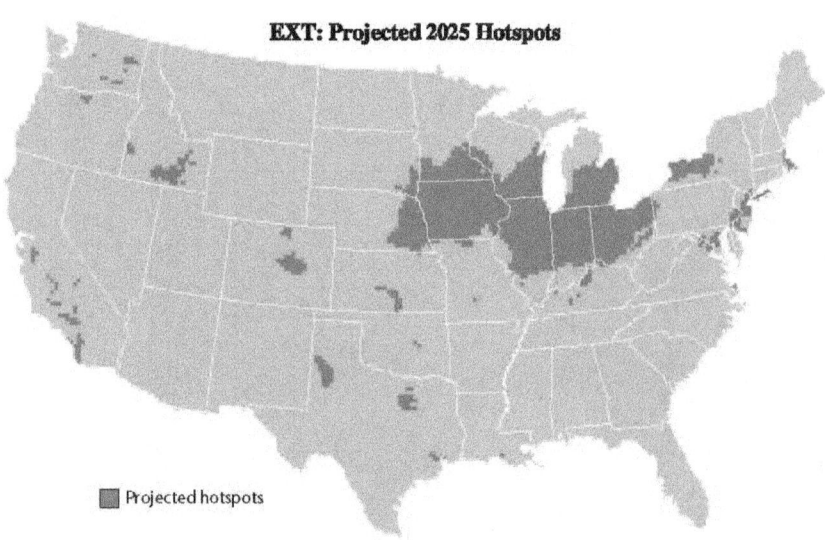

EXT: Projected 2025 Hotspots

Projected hotspots

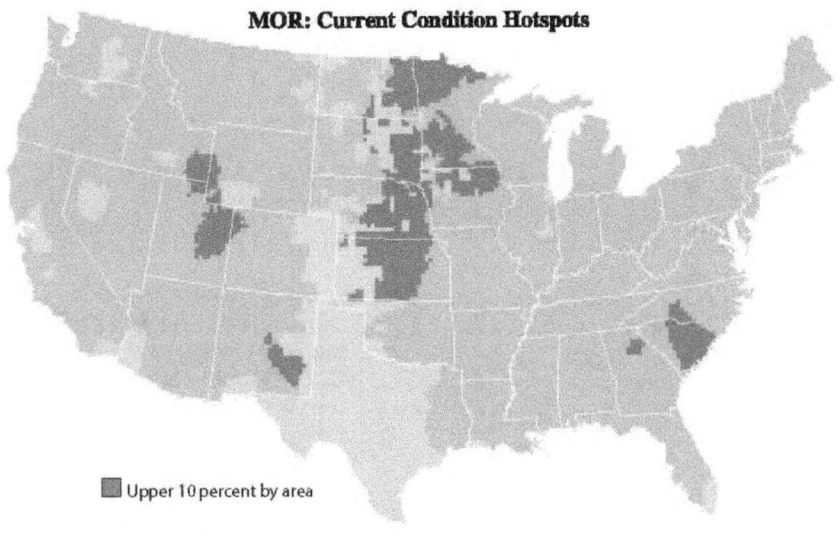

MOR: Current Condition Hotspots

■ Upper 10 percent by area

MOR: False Hotspot Errors

■ False hotspot errors

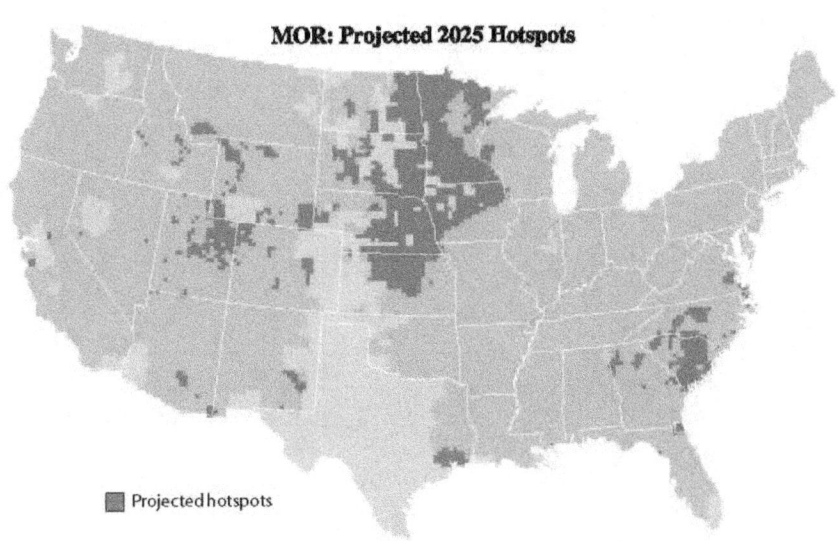

MOR: Projected 2025 Hotspots

■ Projected hotspots

Figure 5. (a) Current Condition Hotspots, (b) False Hotspot Errors from the CART Model, and (c) Projected CART Model Hotspots to 2025 for MOR. The Current Condition Hotspots are the grid cells with the worst 10 percent of the MOR values in the current data set, the False Hotspot Errors are the grid cells that the CART model incorrectly classified as hotspots based on the current values for the independent variables, and the Projected Hotspots are the grid cells that the CART model classified as hotspots based on the projected values of the independent variables.

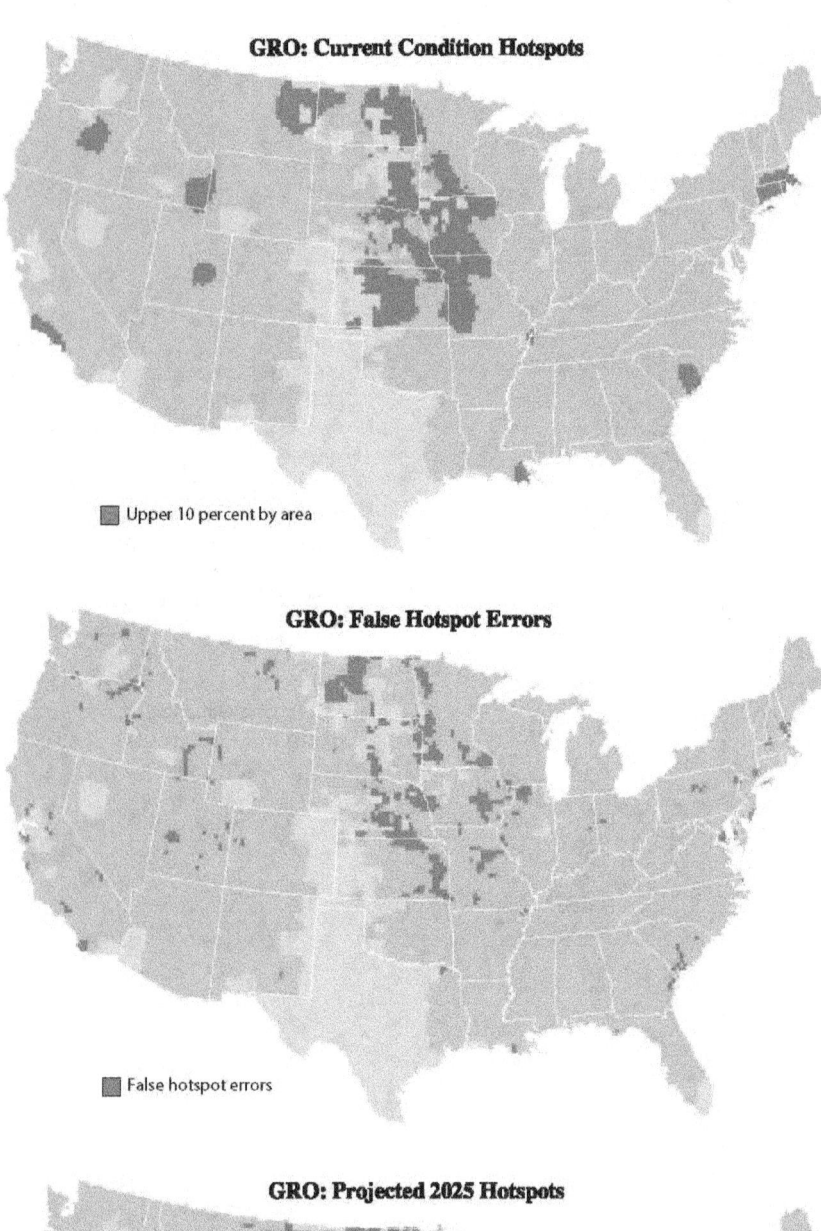

GRO: Current Condition Hotspots

Upper 10 percent by area

GRO: False Hotspot Errors

False hotspot errors

GRO: Projected 2025 Hotspots

Projected hotspots

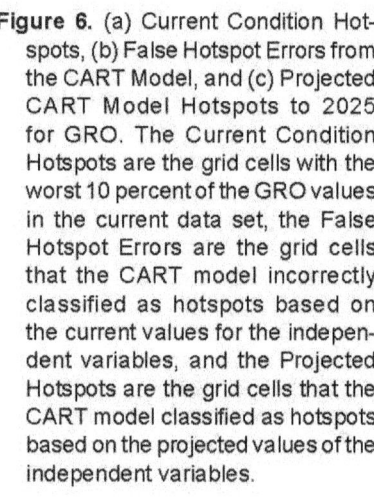

Figure 6. (a) Current Condition Hotspots, (b) False Hotspot Errors from the CART Model, and (c) Projected CART Model Hotspots to 2025 for GRO. The Current Condition Hotspots are the grid cells with the worst 10 percent of the GRO values in the current data set, the False Hotspot Errors are the grid cells that the CART model incorrectly classified as hotspots based on the current values for the independent variables, and the Projected Hotspots are the grid cells that the CART model classified as hotspots based on the projected values of the independent variables.

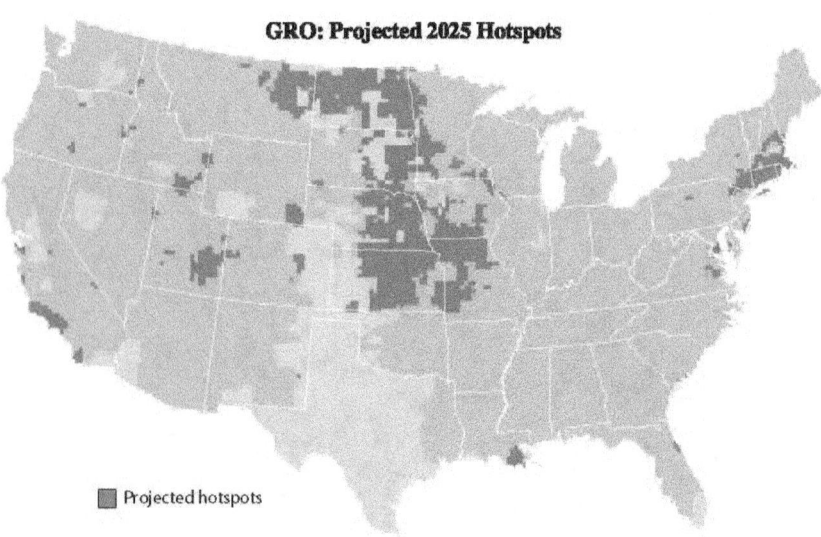

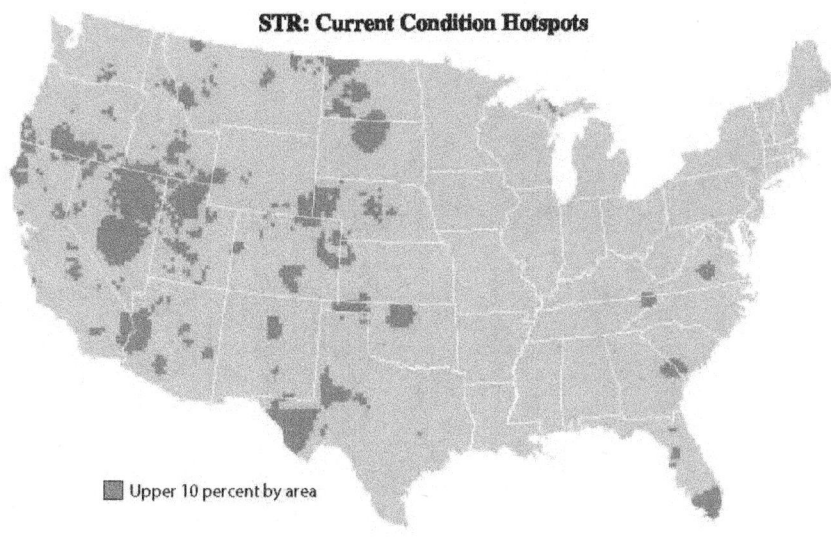

STR: Current Condition Hotspots

☐ Upper 10 percent by area

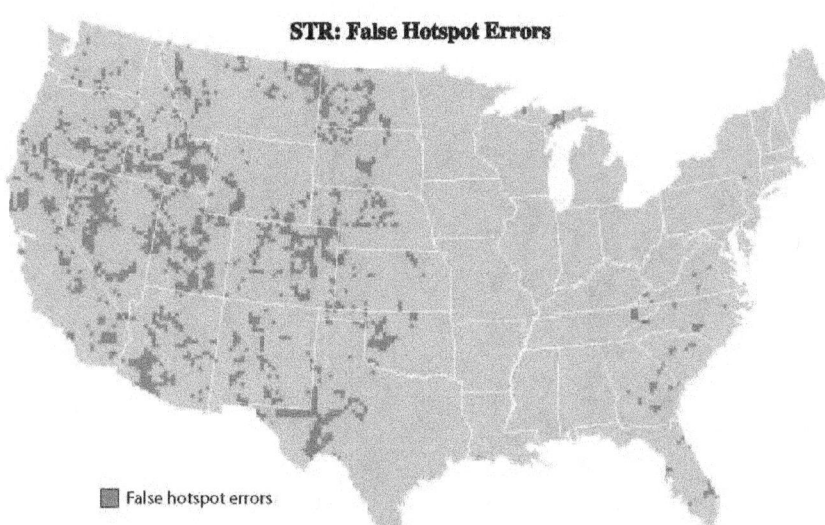

STR: False Hotspot Errors

☐ False hotspot errors

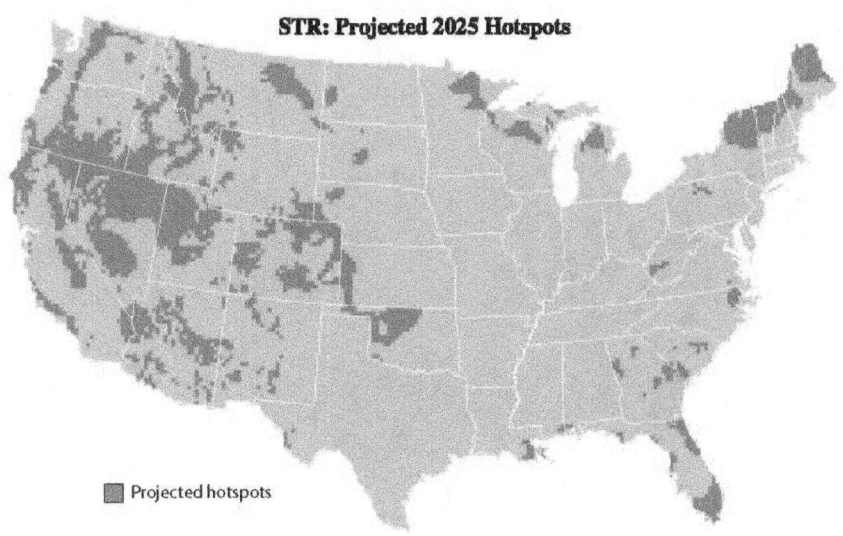

STR: Projected 2025 Hotspots

☐ Projected hotspots

Figure 7. (a) Current Condition Hotspots, (b) False Hotspot Errors from the CART Model, and (c) Projected CART Model Projected Hotspots to 2025 for STR. The Current Condition Hotspots are the grid cells with the worst 10 percent of the STR values in the current data set, the False Hotspot Errors are the grid cells that the CART model incorrectly classified as hotspots based on the current values for the independent variables, and the Projected Hotspots are the grid cells that the CART model classified as hotspots based on the projected values of the independent variables.

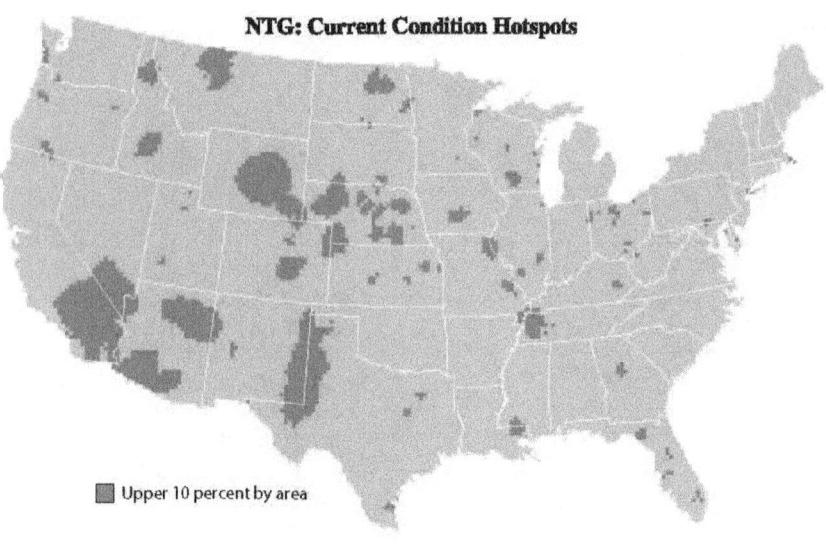

NTG: Current Condition Hotspots

■ Upper 10 percent by area

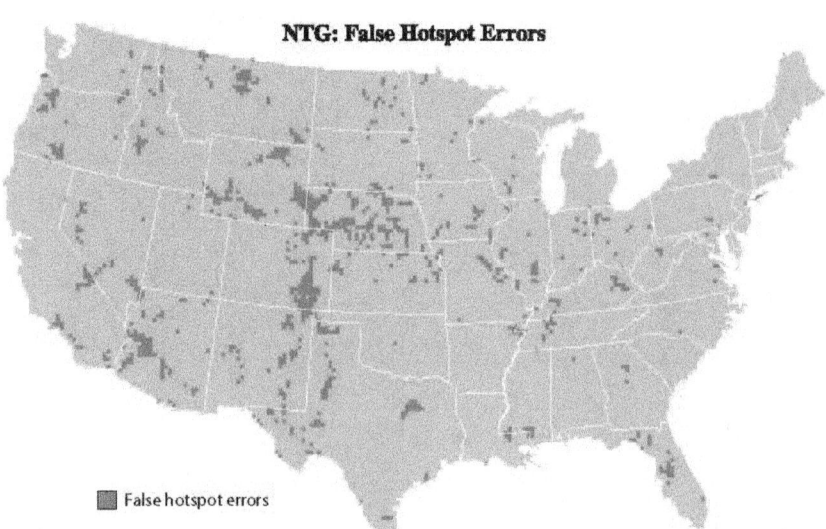

NTG: False Hotspot Errors

■ False hotspot errors

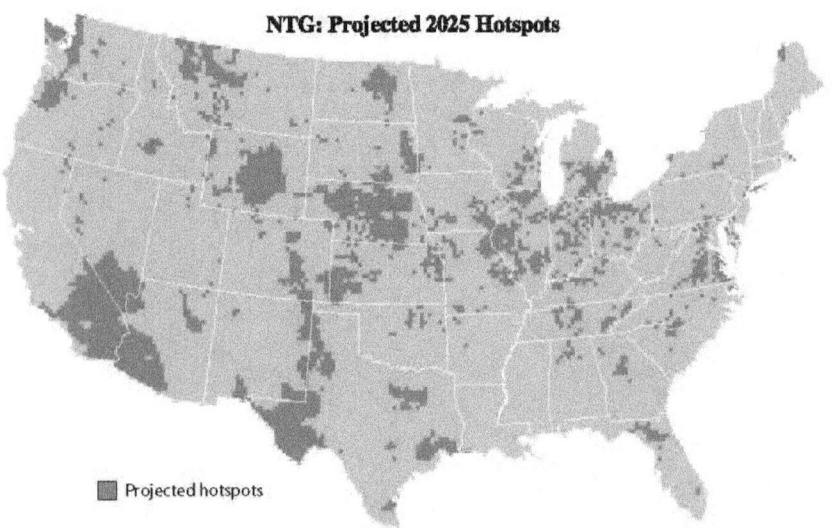

NTG: Projected 2025 Hotspots

■ Projected hotspots

Figure 8. (a) Current Condition Hotspots, (b) False Hotspot Errors from the CART Model, and (c) Projected CART Model Hotspots to 2025 for NTG. The Current Condition Hotspots are the grid cells with the worst 10 percent of the NTG values in the current data set, the False Hotspot Errors are the grid cells that the CART model incorrectly classified as hotspots based on the current values for the independent variables, and the Projected Hotspots are the grid cells that the CART model classified as hotspots based on the projected values of the independent variables.

PHO: Current Condition Hotspots

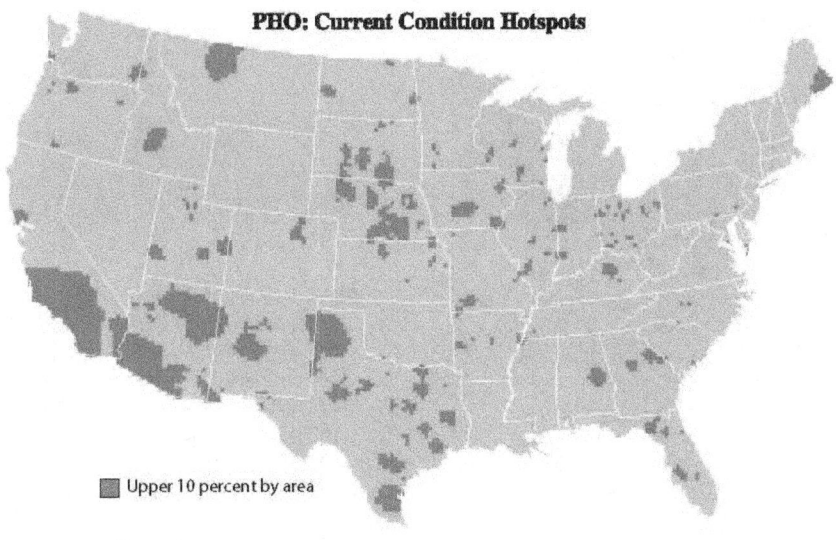

☐ Upper 10 percent by area

Figure 9. (a) Current Condition Hotspots, (b) False Hotspot Errors from the CART Model, and (c) Projected CART Model Hotspots to 2025 for PHO. The Current Condition Hotspots are the grid cells with the worst 10 percent of the PHO values in the current data set, the False Hotspot Errors are the grid cells that the CART model incorrectly classified as hotspots based on the current values for the independent variables, and the Projected Hotspots are the grid cells that the CART model classified as hotspots based on the projected values of the independent variables.

PHO: False Hotspot Errors

☐ False hotspot errors

PHO: Projected 2025 Hotspots

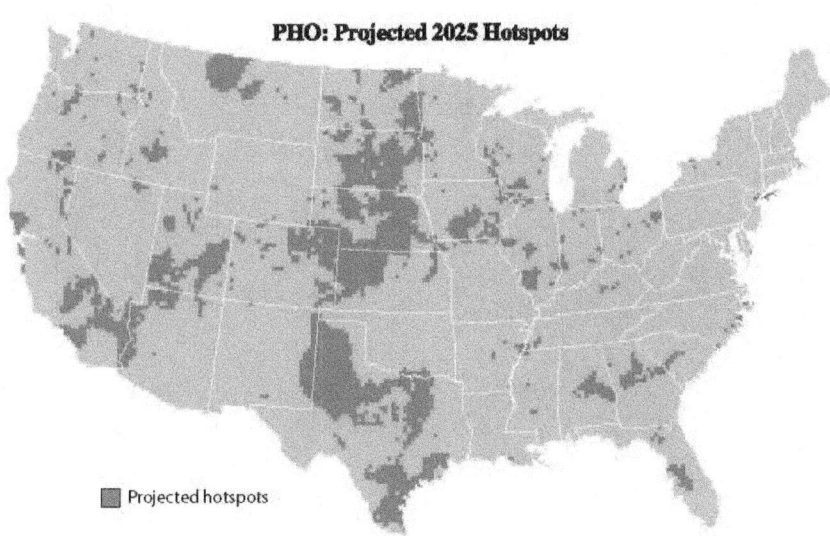

☐ Projected hotspots

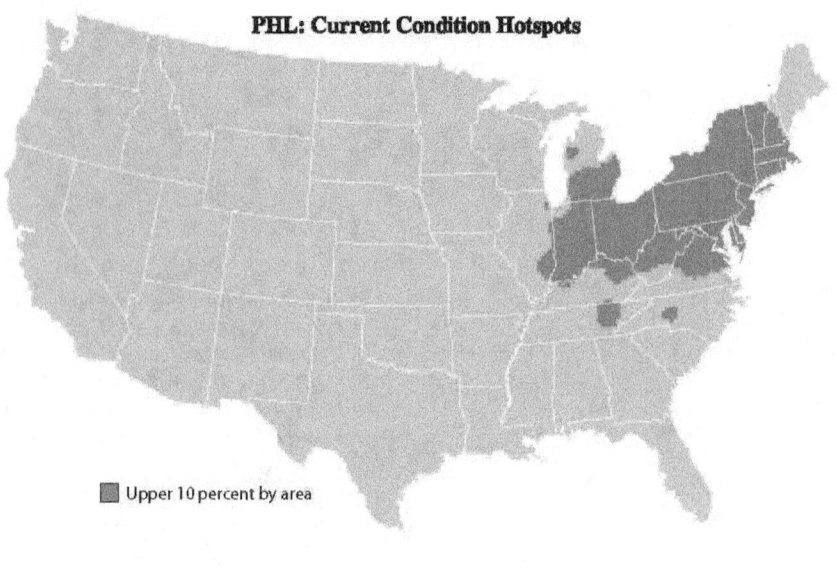

PHL: Current Condition Hotspots

■ Upper 10 percent by area

PHL: False Hotspot Errors

■ False hotspot errors

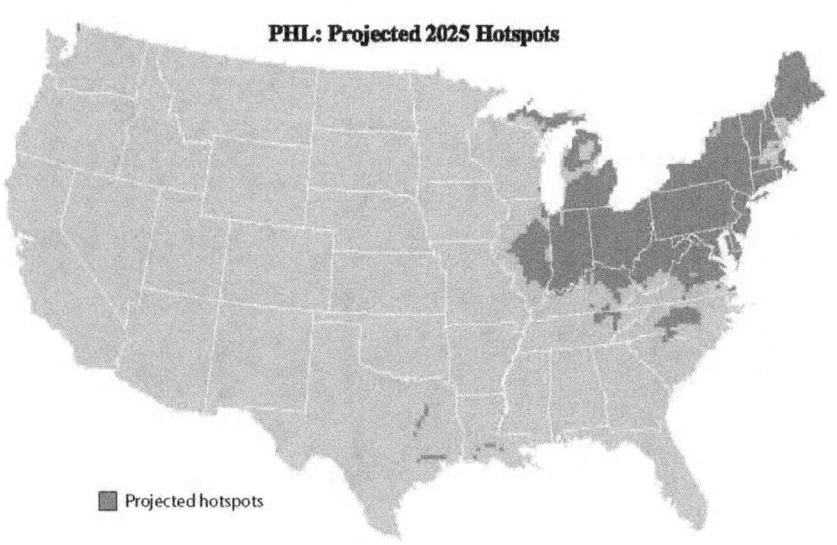

PHL: Projected 2025 Hotspots

■ Projected hotspots

Figure 10. (a) Current Condition Hotspots, (b) False Hotspot Errors from the CART Model, and (c) Projected CART Model Hotspots to 2025 for PHL. The Current Condition Hotspots are the grid cells with the worst 10 percent of the PHL values in the current data set, the False Hotspot Errors are the grid cells that the CART model incorrectly classified as hotspots based on the current values for the independent variables, and the Projected Hotspots are the grid cells that the CART model classified as hotspots based on the projected values of the independent variables.

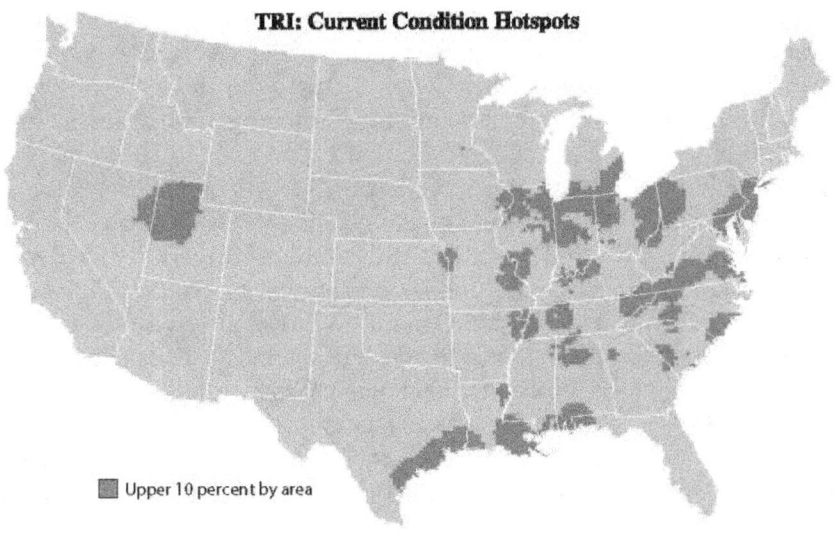

TRI: Current Condition Hotspots

Upper 10 percent by area

TRI: False Hotspot Errors

False hotspot errors

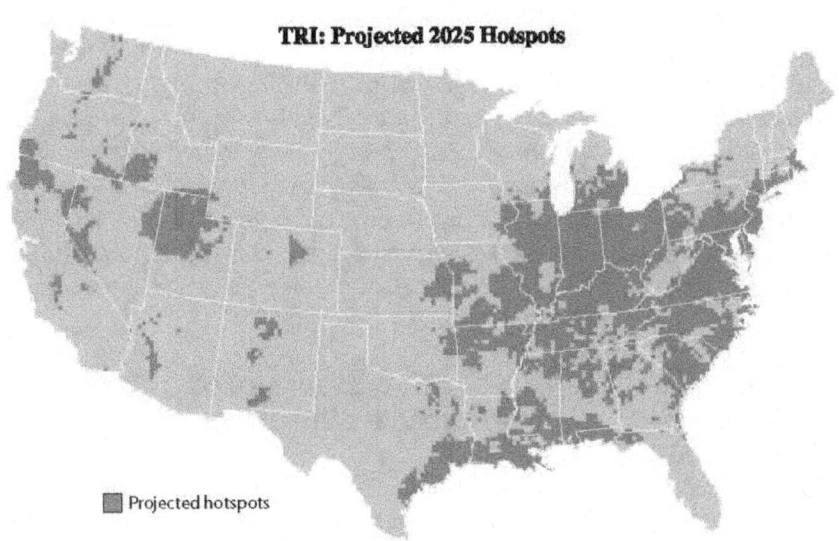

TRI: Projected 2025 Hotspots

Projected hotspots

Figure 11. (a) Current Condition Hotspots, (b) False Hotspot Errors from the CART Model, and (c) Projected CART Model Hotspots to 2025 for TRI. The Current Condition Hotspots are the grid cells with the worst 10 percent of the TRI values in the current data set, the False Hotspot Errors are the grid cells that the CART model incorrectly classified as hotspots based on the current values for the independent variables, and the Projected Hotspots are the grid cells that the CART model classified as hotspots based on the projected values of the independent variables.

Exotic Breeding Birds (EXT)

A common observation in the ecosystem stress literature is that as resource development intensifies there is typically an increase in the abundance of exotic (non-native) species that tolerate human activity (Rapport and others 1985; Pimentel and others 2000). The number of exotic individuals compared to the total number of individuals within some taxonomic group has been proposed as a useful indicator of ecosystem health (National Research Council 2000) and has been used recently with bird monitoring data as a broad-scale indicator of ecosystem condition (Hof and others 1999a; Sieg and others 1999).

The proportion of exotic species currently comprising the bird community is especially prominent throughout the upper Midwest (figure 4a). There are some smaller, isolated current condition hotspots in the mid-Atlantic region, Texas, Idaho, southern California, and the Pacific Northwest. The false hotspot errors from the CART model (figure 4b) closely surround the current EXT hotspots. The CART model projections (figure 4c) indicate stability in the large Midwestern hotspot, a reduction in the hotspot area in the mid-Atlantic region, and new hotspots in Colorado, Kansas, Oklahoma, and Texas.

Timber Mortality (MOR)

A less well-studied aspect of ecosystem condition indicators involves the effect of various stressors on disease incidence (Rapport and others 1985). One group of host organisms where there has been a number of studies examining the relationship between stress and disease is trees (Manion 1981). The ultimate stress that predisposes a tree to death may be quite different from the proximate mortality factor. For example, Dahlsten and Rowney (1980) found that air pollution rendered ponderosa pine (*Pinus ponderosa*) more vulnerable to insect infestation. Our interest here is not to attribute cause to increasing tree mortality, but to simply use the mortality rate as an indicator of some undefined stress or set of stresses. Because the data for this indicator are limited to timberland, we excluded those counties that had no timberland (light gray areas in figures 5a-c). Timberland is defined as "Forest land that is producing or capable of producing in excess of 20 cubic feet per acre per year of wood at culmination of mean annual increment..." and is not withdrawn from timber utilization by statute or administrative regulation (Bechtold and Patterson 2005:84).

High mortality rates for timberland currently occur in four distinct areas throughout the country (figure 5a). Notable areas of clustering occur in the Great Plains, the coastal plain and piedmont regions of South Carolina and North Carolina (and a bit in Georgia), New Mexico, and the interior West. The ultimate cause of the increased mortality is likely very different in each of these hotspots. The false hotspot errors from the CART model (figure 5b) are closely associated with the current hotspots. The CART model projections (figure 5c) indicate a strong reduction in the New Mexico hotspot, a diffusion of the Interior West hotspot, a concentration of the Great Plains hotspot, and some diffusion of the Southeastern hotspot. Small new hotspots are projected in the Gulf Coast region of Texas, Arizona, California, and Florida

Timber Growth (GRO)

When under stress, trees alter their normal pattern of carbon allocation by decreasing stem growth (Waring 1987). Consequently, reductions in tree growth will often precede a detectable change in tree mortality. Although timber growth and mortality rates are expected to be correlated, reductions in timber growth may actually serve as an early warning sign, relative to timber mortality, of ecosystem stress. Again, because the data for this indicator are limited to timberland, we excluded those counties that had no timberland (light gray areas in figures 6a-c).

The results for GRO (in figures 6a-c) are quite similar to those discussed for MOR (note that GRO is defined as 1 minus the ratio of actual growth to potential growth). The current condition hotspots (figure 6a) are, if anything, slightly more diffuse than timber mortality with additional hotpots in the Northeast, Northwest, and California. The false hotspot errors from the CART model (figure 6b) are generally associated with the current hotspots but the errors are scattered across the East Coast and the West. The CART projections (figure 6c) indicate a scattering of the hotspots across the West, some expansion of the Great Plains and the Northeast hotspots, and essentially a disappearance of the hotspot in South Carolina.

Negative Deviations From Mean Streamflows (STR)

Human alteration of land cover has obvious direct effects on terrestrial systems. Those alterations coupled with increasing human populations also affect aquatic systems through their influence on the hydrologic cycle. Clearing of land for agriculture or urban development can increase the amount of water reaching water courses by reducing transpiration, interception, and infiltration (Arnold and Gibbons 1996; Goudie 2000; Weng 2001); however, we assume that the effects of concern from agricultural development and human population growth are the reductions in stream flows that result from increased water withdrawals (Brown 2000).

The current condition hotspots for STR (figure 7a) are spread across the western half of the country, with a few areas in the Southeast. The false hotspot errors from the CART model (figure 7b) are generally associated with the current hotspots but the errors are rather extensive in some areas. The projections from the CART model (figure 7c) indicate some expansion of the hotspots in the West, as well as new hotspots in the Great Lakes states and the far Northeast. The projected hotspots in the Southeast shift somewhat relative to the current condition hotspots, and the hotspots in Texas all but disappear.

Total Nitrogen in Surface Waters (NTG)

In disturbed systems there is often a loss of nutrients through leaching and soil erosion (Likens and others 1978). Chemical cycles become leaky causing elevated nutrient delivery and accumulation in aquatic systems (Rapport and others 1985; Magdoff and others 1997; National Research Council 2000). Furthermore, nutrient loads in aquatic systems can become elevated due to direct input from sewage, animal waste, and synthetic fertilizer application (Goudie 2000). Nitrogen is an important element in plant and animal nutrition, but elevated levels can have detrimental effects on ecosystem function and human health (National Research Council 2000). We use a measure of total nitrogen in surface waters (also called total Kjeldahl nitrogen) as described in Mueller and others (1995:7).

Current areas of high total nitrogen levels (figure 8a) appear diffusely across the country with some spatial clustering in the Interior West, the Midwest, and the arid Southwest. The false hotspot errors from the CART model (figure 8b) are generally associated with the current hotspots but the errors are also rather scattered in some areas. The CART model projections (figure 8c) indicate intensification of stress in the Midwest, the Pacific Northwest, the Southwest, and the far East.

Texas and Nebraska exhibit particularly large hotspot expansions.

Total Phosphorous in Surface Waters (PHO)

Phosphorous concentrations are another common indicator of water quality (O'Neill and others 1997) that can alter ecosystem condition through their accelerating effect on eutrophication (Goudie 2000). Elevated phosphorous levels are caused by many of the same agents as nitrogen—namely sewage, animal waste, fertilizers, and detergents. Because of the shared origins, phosphorous levels are expected to be correlated with nitrogen levels. However, there are reasons why these two nutrients are not necessarily redundant indictors of water quality. Phosphorous is less mobile than nitrogen, adhering strongly to soil constituents. Consequently, phosphorous levels in surface waters are affected by the type, texture, and level of organic matter in the soil (National Research Council 2000). We use a measure of total phosphorous (mg of P/L) as described in Mueller and others (1995:7).

Areas of high total phosphorous currently appear diffusely across the country (figure 9a). There is some geographic similarity with nitrogen—namely concentration of analysis grid cells supporting high levels of phosphorous in the upper Midwest, the Southwest, the Interior West, and the Gulf Coast. The false hotspot errors from the CART model (figure 9b) are generally associated with the current hotspots but the errors show some general scattering as well. The projections from the CART model (figure 9c) indicate a dramatic increase in stress in the Midwest from Texas to the Dakotas. Increases are also evident in the Southeast and Utah, with decreases in hotspot area in the arid Southwest. The hotspot in Maine also disappears.

Ph in Precipitation (PHL)

Chemical compounds can also impact ecosystem condition through the process of atmospheric deposition. Increased acidification of precipitation (higher loads of H^+) is prominent among these concerns (Likens and Bormann 1974). Sulphur oxides and nitrogen oxides from fossil-fuel combustion are the primary compounds causing increased acidity in precipitation, and its effects on the structure and function of ecosystems are potentially widespread—causing, among other things, accelerated leaching of soil nutrients, increased solubility of toxic heavy metals, reductions in fish and algae diversity, slower growth in forests, and reduced seed germination (Goudie 2000).

The current condition hotspots for PHL (figure 10a) are essentially restricted to the Northeast. The false hotspot errors from the CART model (figure 10b) are on the margin of the current hotspot cluster but are quite noticeable in Maine, Illinois, and the Great Lakes States. The projections from the CART model (figure 10c) indicate a continuance of this area of stress in the Northeast, with some expansion into the areas identified as false hotspot errors in figure 10b. Whether this is model error or a tenable projection is difficult to assess (as discussed previously).

Total Toxic Chemical Releases to the Environment (TRI)

Chemical pollutants can take many forms. Previous indicators have been targeted to a restricted set of compounds. This indicator attempts to capture changes in ecosystem condition caused by a much broader suite of contaminants. The Toxics Release Inventory contains information on the releases of nearly 650 chemical categories to the air, water, and land. Because of the diversity of contaminants and their widely varying toxicities, it is difficult to outline generally the ecosystem effects stemming from these pollutants.

The current condition hotspots for TRI (figure 11a) are spread throughout the eastern half of the country (with notable exceptions in the far Northeast and Southeast). There is also a large current hotspot in Utah. The false hotspot errors from the CART model (figure 11b) are generally associated with the current hotspots but the errors also appear in a few areas quite separated from the current condition hotspots. The CART model projections (figure 11c) indicate a significant intensification of the hotspots in the East, as well as many new (and smaller) hotspot areas in the West.

Overlays of the Projected Hotspots

Figure 12 presents an "overlay" of the individual indicator projected hotspots. By this, we mean that figure 12 shows the number of hotspots that were projected to occur in each grid cell across the country. Moving from east to west, the first noteworthy area of projected hotspot

Number of Coincident Projected 2025 Hotspots

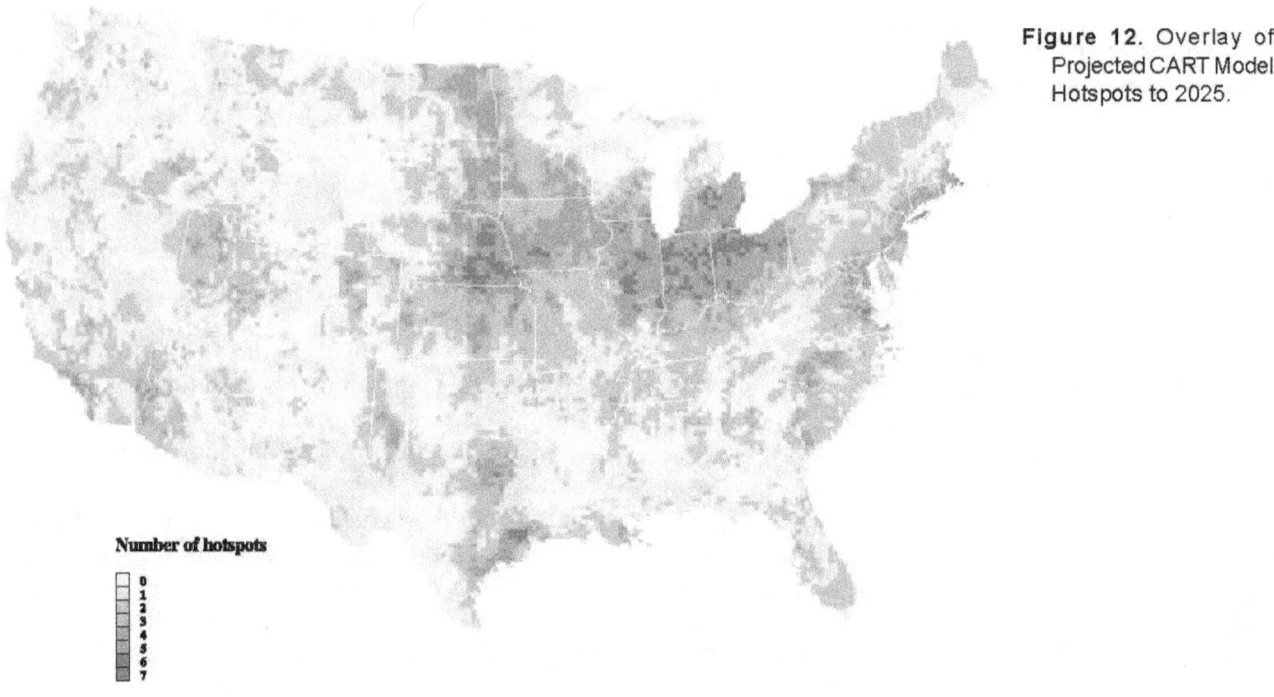

Figure 12. Overlay of Projected CART Model Hotspots to 2025.

Number of hotspots

0
1
2
3
4
5
6
7

concentration is on the Atlantic seaboard, running from South Carolina, through the North Carolina piedmont, to Massachusetts. The most expansive concentration of projected hotspots includes a broad area through the Midwest extending from Ohio in the east, to the till plains of Iowa and western Nebraska in the west, south into Kansas, and north into Minnesota and South Dakota. Three much smaller concentrations appear in Texas, around the Houston area, the Dallas-Fort Worth area, and in western Texas around Lubbock and Amarillo. Additional areas with high concentrations of projected hotspots include the Front Range of Colorado, the Wasatch Range of Utah, the area around Las Vegas, and southern California. Additional areas with two or three projected hotspots are located throughout the West, the Northeast, Florida, and the large area south of the Great Lakes states.

The overall picture in figure 12 is very different from that depicted in Hof and others (1999a, b). We attribute this to at least three factors. First, the hotspots in Hof and others (1999a, b) were defined as those grid cells that had the greatest degree of change in an indicator over the projection period. Here, the hotspots are defined according to the actual magnitude of the projected condition as it compares to the definition of the current condition hotspots. Second, the hotspots in Hof and others (1999a, b) were based on the worst 5 percent whereas a 10 percent threshold is used here. Thus, the hotspots were defined in a totally different way in the two studies. Third, the indicators in this study are quite different than those in the previous study. In Hof and others (1999a, b), the indicators were dominated by threatened and endangered (T and E) species indicators, while the indicators here include a broader emphasis, including such factors as water and air pollution, forest growth and mortality, and more general measures of wildlife habitat and community structure. In this sense, the current indicators better represent those indicators suggested in ongoing efforts to evaluate ecosystem conditions (see for example Rapport and others 1985; Coulombe 1995; National Research Council 2000). Clearly, we cannot draw any conclusions from comparing the results of the two studies. Looking only at the 10 indicators in this GTR, however, it is clear that different indicators paint a different picture of environmental stress. In the individual indicator results section, we discuss why each indicator might be of some use in assessing environmental stress. We would interpret all of our results in light of those more specific descriptions. The overlay in figure 12 is just intended to provide a summary of the indicators analyzed in this study, not as a comprehensive picture of environmental stress in general.

Conclusion

The RPA directs the Forest Service to prepare broad-scaled evaluations of the current status and condition of natural resources, and to anticipate future resource conditions based on trend projections. One concern in meeting this mandate is that evaluation of each resource area independently (for example, timber, forage, wildlife, and recreation) runs the risk of developing conflicting resource management policy—benefiting one resource to the detriment of others. This report represents an attempt to consider many indicators of resource condition simultaneously for the purpose of identifying those areas of the country where ecosystem condition appears problematic. We delineated those problem areas based on the coincident occurrence of indicator values defined to represent the worst condition and defined these as hotspots.

Classification tree analysis was shown to be potentially useful as a hotspot classification tool. Even when limiting the model to explanatory variables that are projected at a geographically specific level, the ability of CART models to identify areas of relative poor ecosystem condition was still fairly good.

With the projection model, we identified potential hotspots in 10 condition indicators for forests and rangelands based on projected changes in land use/cover variables as well as human population. We avoided any interpretations that suggest actual causation because the methods used identify only patterns of association between response and explanatory variables, not cause-effect relationships. Thus, these potential hotspots should be viewed only as candidates for areas of significant change. One policy implication that does seem to be fairly tenable is that the projected hotspot areas for the indicators included in this study do not coincide extensively with National Forest System lands. Thus, addressing the areas of ecosystem stress identified in figure 12 will most likely require cooperation with state and private land owners. This analysis is clearly exploratory in nature, however, and all results reported are tentative. Hopefully, the results will serve to focus additional study in potentially high priority areas, both in terms of research and planning analysis effort. Focused, indicator-by-indicator analyses are expected to lead to better understanding of the potential causes of these broad-scale patterns of ecosystem condition. Further research is clearly needed in developing the methods for studies such as this one, which can serve the purpose of the triage in large scale planning efforts.

References

Alig, R. J.; Plantiga, A. J.; Ahn, S.; Kline, J. D. 2003. Land use changes involving forestry in the United States: 1952 to 1997, with projections to 2050. Gen. Tech. Rep. PNW-GTR-587. Portland, OR: U.S. Department of Agriculture, Forest Service, Pacific Northwest Research Station. 92 p.

Allen, T. F. H.; Hoekstra, T. W. 1992. Toward a unified ecology. New York: Columbia University Press. 384 p.

Arnold, C. L.; Gibbons, C. J. 1996. Impervious surface coverage: the emergence of a key environmental indicator. Journal of the American Planning Association. 62: 243-258.

Barnes, S. L. 1964. A technique for maximizing details in numerical weather map analysis. Journal of Applied Meteorology. 3: 396-409.

Barrett, G. W.; Van Dyne, G. M.; Odum, E. P. 1976. Stress ecology. BioScience. 26: 192-194.

Bechtold, W. A.; Patterson, P. L., eds. 2005. The enhanced forest inventory and analysis program—national sampling design and estimation procedures. Gen. Tech. Rep. SRS-80. Asheville, NC: U.S. Department of Agriculture, Forest Service, Southern Research Station. 85 p.

Bender, D. J.; Contreras, T. A.; Fahrig, L. 1998. Habitat loss and population decline: a meta-analysis of the patch size effect. Ecology. 79: 517-533.

Breiman, L.; Friedman, J. H.; Olshen, R. A.; Stone, C. J. 1984. Classification and regression trees. Belmont, CA: Wadsworth. 358 p.

Brown, T. C. 2000. Projecting U.S. freshwater withdrawals. Water Resources Research. 36: 769-780.

Coulombe, M. J. 1995. Sustaining the world's forests: the Santiago Agreement. Journal of Forestry. 93: 18-21.

Cressie, A. C. N. 1991. Statistics for spatial data. New York: John Wiley & Sons, Inc. 900 p.

Dahlsten, D. L.; Rowney, D. L. 1980. Influence of air pollution on population dynamics of forest insects and on tree mortality. In: Symposium on effects of air pollution on Mediterranean and temperate forest ecosystems. Gen. Tech. Rep. PSW-43. Berkeley, CA: U.S. Department of Agriculture, Forest Service, Pacific Southwest Forest and Range Experiment Station: 125-131.

Daily, G. C. 1997. Nature's services: societal dependence on natural ecosystems. Washington, DC: Island Press. 392 p.

De'ath, G.; Fabricius, K. E. 2000. Classification and regression trees: a powerful yet simple technique for ecological data analysis. Ecology. 81: 3178-3192.

DellaSala, D. A.; Staus, N. L.; Strittholt, J. R.; Hackman, A.; Iacobelli, A. 2001. An updated protected areas database for the United States and Canada. Natural Areas Journal. 21: 124-135.

Flather, C. H.; Bevers, M. 2002. Patchy reaction diffusion and population abundance: the relative importance of habitat amount and arrangement. American Naturalist. 159: 40-56.

Goudie, A. 2000. The human impact on the natural environment, 5th ed. Cambridge, MA: MIT Press. 511 p.

Haining, R. 1990. Spatial data analysis in the social and environmental sciences. Cambridge, MA: Cambridge University Press. 409 p.

Hall, C. A. S.; Day, J. W., eds. 1977. Ecosystem modeling in theory and practice. New York: John Wiley & Sons, Inc. 684 p.

Hansen, M. H.; Frieswyk, T.; Glover, J. F.; Kelly, J. F. 1992. Eastwide forest inventory data base: user's manual. Gen. Tech. Rep. NC-GTR-151. St. Paul, MN: U.S. Department of Agriculture, Forest Service, North Central Forest Experiment Station. 48 p.

Harrison, S.; Bruna, E. 1999. Habitat fragmentation and large-scale conservation: what do we know for sure? Ecography. 22: 225-232.

Heinz Center. 2002. The state of the Nation's ecosystems. Washington, DC: The H. John Heinz Center for Science, Economics, and the Environment. 288 p.

Hof, J.; Baltic, T. 1988. Forest and rangeland resource interactions: a supporting technical document for the 1989 RPA Assessment. Gen. Tech. Rep. RM-156. Fort Collins, CO: U.S. Department of Agriculture, Forest Service, Rocky Mountain Forest and Range Experiment Station. 31 p.

Hof, J.; Davies, S.; Baltic, T. 1998. Production functions for large-scale forest and range condition indicators. Socio-Economic Planning Sciences. 32: 295-308.

Hof, J.; Flather, C.; Baltic, T.; and Davies, S. 1999a. Projections of forest and rangeland condition indicators for a national assessment. Environmental Management. 24: 383-398.

Hof, J.; Flather, C.; Baltic, T.; Davies S. 1999b. National projections of forest and rangeland condition indicators: a technical document supporting the 1999 USDA Forest Service RPA assessment. Gen. Tech. Rep. PNW-GTR-442. Portland, OR: U.S. Department of Agriculture, Forest Service, Pacific Northwest Research Station. 57 p.

Kittel, T. G. F.; Royle, J. A.; Daly, C.; Rosenbloom, N. A.; Gibson, W. P.; Fisher, H. H.; Schimel, D. S.; Berliner, L. M.; VEMAP 2 Participants. 1997. A gridded historical (1895-1993) bioclimate dataset for the conterminous United States. In: Proceedings of the 10th conference on applied climatology. Boston, MA: American Meteorological Society: 219-222.

Küchler, A. W. 1964. Manual to accompany the map—potential natural vegetation of the conterminous United States. Special Publ. No. 36. New York: American Geographical Society.

Küchler, A. W. 1993. Potential natural vegetation of the conterminous United States. Global Ecosystems Database, Version 2. Boulder, CO: NOAA, National Geophysical Data Center.

Laurance, W. F. 2000. Do edge effects occur over large spatial scales? Trends in Ecology and Evolution. 15: 134-135.

Likens, G. E.; Bormann, F. H. 1974. Acid rain: a serious regional environmental problem. Science. 184: 1176-1179.

Likens, G. E.; Bormann, F. H.; Pierce, R. S.; Reiners, W. A. 1978. Recovery of a deforested ecosystem. Science. 199: 492-496.

Loreau, M.; Naeem, S.; Inchausti, P.; Bengtsson, J.; Grime, J. P.; Hector, A.; Hooper, D. U.; Huston, M. A.; Raffaelli, D.; Schmid, B.; Tilman, D.; Wardle, D. A. 2001. Biodiversity and ecosystem functioning: current knowledge and future challenges. Science. 294: 804-808.

Magdoff, F.; Lanyon, L.; Liebhardt, B. 1997. Nutrient cycling, transformations, and flows: implications for a more sustainable agriculture. Advances in Agronomy. 60: 1-73.

Manion, P. D. 1981. Tree disease concepts. Englewood Cliffs, NJ: Prentice-Hall. 399 p.

Mittelhammer, R. C.; Matulich, S. C.; Bushaw, D. 1981. On implicit forms of multiproduct-multifactor production functions. American Journal of Agricultural Economics. 63: 164-168.

Mueller, D. K.; Hamilton, P. A.; Helsel, D. R.; Hitt, K. J.; Ruddy, B. C. 1995. Nutrients in ground water and surface water of the United States—an analysis of data through 1992. Water Resources Investigation Report 95-4031. Denver, CO: U.S. Geological Survey.

Muradian, R. 2001. Ecological thresholds: a survey. Ecological Economics. 38: 7-24.

National Research Council. 2000. Ecological indicators for the nation. Washington, DC: National Academy Press. 180 p.

Nobel, I. R.; Dirzo, R. 1997. Forests as human-dominated ecosystems. Science. 277: 522-525.

O'Neill, R. V.; Hunsaker, C. T.; Jones, K. B.; Riitters, K. H.; Wickham, J. D.; Schwarz, P.; Goodman, I. A.; Jackson, B.; Baillargeon, W. S. 1997. Monitoring environmental quality at the landscape scale. BioScience. 47: 513-519.

Pimentel, D.; Lach, L.; Zuniga, R.; Morrison, D. 2000. Environmental and economic costs of nonindigenous species in the United States. BioScience. 50: 53-65.

Rapport, D. J.; Regier, H. A.; Hutchinson, T. C. 1985. Ecosystem behavior under stress. American Naturalist. 125: 617-640.

Ripley, B. D. 1981. Spatial statistics. New York: John Wiley & Sons, Inc. 252 p.

Riitters K. H. 2004. Criteria 1: Conservation of biological diversity. Indicator 5: Fragmentation of forest types. In: D. Darr, coordinator. Data report: a supplement to the national report on sustainable forests—2003. FS-766A. Washington, DC: U.S. Department of Agriculture, Forest Service. Available: http://www.fs.fed.us/research/sustain/.

Robertson, F. D. 1992. Ecosystem management of the National Forests and Grasslands. 1330-1 policy letter. June 4, 1992. On file at: U.S. Department of Agriculture, Forest Service, Washington, DC.

Robertson, G. P. 2000. Geostatistics for the Environmental Sciences. GS+ User's Guide, Version 5. Plainwell, MI: Gamma Design Software. 200 p.

Saunders, D. A.; Hobbs, R. J.; Margules, C. R. 1991. Biological consequences of ecosystem fragmentation: a review. Conservation Biology. 5: 18-32.

Schimel, D.; Melillo, J.; Tian, H.; McGuire, A. D.; Kicklighter, D.; Kittel, T.; Rosenbloom, N.; Running, S.; Thorton, P.; Ojima, D.; Parton, W.; Kelly, R.; Sykes, M.; Neilson, R.; B. Rizzo, B. 2000. Contribution of increasing CO_2 and climate to carbon storage by ecosystems of the United States. Science. 287: 2004-2006.

Sieg, C. H.; Flather, C. H.; McCanny, S. 1999. Recent biodiversity patterns in the Great Plains: implications for restoration and management. Great Plains Research. 9: 277-313.

Steinburg, D.; Colla, P. 2000. CART 4.0—Classification and Regression Trees. San Diego, CA: Salford Systems.

U.S. Department of Agriculture, Forest Service. 1989. An analysis of the land base situation in the United States: 1989-2040. A technical document supporting the 1989 USDA Forest Service RPA assessment. Gen. Tech. Rep. RM-181. Fort Collins, CO: U.S. Department of Agriculture, Forest Service, Rocky Mountain Forest and Range Experiment Station. 76 p.

U.S. Department of Agriculture, Forest Service. 1990. The Forest Service program for forest and rangeland resources: a long-term strategic plan. Washington, DC: U.S. Department of Agriculture, Forest Service.

U.S. Department of Agriculture, Forest Service. 1994. RPA assessment of the forest and rangeland situation in the United States–1993 update. Forest Resource Report No. 27. Washington, DC: U.S. Department of Agriculture, Forest Service. 75 p.

U.S. Department of Agriculture, Forest Service. 1995. The Forest Service program for forest and rangeland resources: A long-term strategic plan. Draft 1995 RPA program. Washington, DC: U.S. Department of Agriculture, Forest Service.

U.S. Department of Agriculture, Forest Service. 2001. 2000 RPA assessment of forest and rangelands. FS-687, February 2001. Washington, DC: U.S. Department of Agriculture, Forest Service, 78 p.

Vitousek, P. M.; Mooney, H. A.; Lubchenco, J.; Melillo, J. M. 1997. Human domination of Earth's ecosystems. Science. 277: 494-499.

Waring, R. H. 1987. Characteristics of trees predisposed to die. BioScience. 37: 569-574.

Weng, Q. 2001. Modeling urban growth effects on surface runoff with the integration of remote sensing and GIS. Environmental Management. 28: 737-748.

Woods and Poole Economics, Inc. 2003. 2003 Woods and Poole data on CD-ROM: complete U.S. database. Washington, DC: Woods and Poole Economics, Inc.

Woudenberg, S. W.; Farrenkopf, T. O. 1995. Westwide forest inventory data base: user's manual. Gen. Tech. Rep. INT-GTR-317. Odgen, UT: U.S. Department of Agriculture, Forest Service, Intermountain Research Station. 67 p.

Yorke, T. H.; Williams, O. O. 1991. Design of a National Water Information System by the U.S. Geological Survey. In: Proceedings of the 7th international conference on interactive information and processing systems for meteorology, hydrology, and oceanography. New Orleans, LA: American Meteorological Society: 284-288.

Appendix A: Variable Descriptions and Data Sources

The database includes 10 response variables representing forest and rangeland conditions. Based on the previous discussion, we included 21 explanatory variables including seven measures of human activity (including six land use/land cover types and human population), two variables that relate to federal/non-federal ownership, a categorical variable to account for ecoregional differences, and 11 measures of climate and topographic variation. Because of data availability, only the coterminous United States is included. The database contains observations on each variable by uniform grid cell. There are 17,000 cells in the database, and each cell is approximately 21,376.5 meters square (45,695.5 ha) in size. The size of the grid cells was based on a univariate analysis of the range in county sizes, such that our grid cell size corresponds to the 5 percent quantile level of county sizes (only 5 percent of the counties in the coterminous United States are smaller than our cell size). Our 17,000-cell grid will be referred to here as the "analysis grid."

The indicators of forest and rangeland condition were chosen because of their likelihood of being affected by human activity, their availability, and their consistency (as possible) with the Montréal Process indicators (for a description of Montréal Process indicators see Coulombe [1995]). Data were obtained from numerous sources in formats ranging from digital spatial databases to highly aggregated county data and micro data with many sample points. Most of the data had to be reformatted or otherwise processed and synthesized to be consistent with the data structure requirements of the analytical approach. In the case of micro data with many sampling points, analysis grid cell observations were obtained by "kriging" to the cell centroid (see Ripley [1981]; Haining [1990]; Cressie [1991] for a detailed discussion of kriging and geostatistical techniques in general).

The data for this analysis is described, with sources, below:

Variable	Description	Source
Condition Indicators:		
EDG	A measure of total linear edge between natural land cover (forest, shrub, grass) and anthropogenic land use (developed, disturbed, agriculture) within a 7.5 km x 7.5 km square analysis unit gridded at 30 m resolution. In a GIS procedure, the analysis grid cells were defined as "zones" and zonal means of total linear edge were calculated based on the 30 m resolution cells that fell in each zone. The broad land cover classes are defined as follows: forest includes deciduous, evergreen, mixed, and woody wetland; shrub includes shrubland; grass includes grasslands/herbaceous and herbaceous wetland; developed includes low intensity residential, high intensity residential, commercial/industrial/transportation, and urban/recreational	Edge-based measure of fragmentation, 2002: Data made available on CD-ROM in ASCII and SAS format / prepared by USDA Forest Service, Research Triangle Park, NC: Forestry Sciences Lab, Forest Health Monitoring (SRS-4803), 2002. Fragmentation databases will be available at http://www.srs.fs.usda.gov/4803/landscapes/index.html. See also Riitters (2004).

	grasses; disturbed includes bare rock/sand/clay, quarries/strip mines/gravel pits, and transitional; agriculture includes row crops, small grains, pasture/hay, fallow, and orchards/vineyards/other.	
PCH	A measure of average patch size (area weighted average) within a 7.5 km x 7.5 km square analysis unit gridded at 30 m resolution. These analysis units were overlaid on land-cover maps for the lower 48 states from the National Land Cover Data (NLCD) database. A patch was defined as a block of contiguous (in the 4 cardinal directions) natural land cover (forest, shrub, grass). The average patch size for each analysis unit was estimated for the land cover type that was expected to be the potential natural vegetation within the analysis unit based on an overlay of the analysis unit grid with a Küchler PNV coverage (Küchler 1964). In a GIS procedure, the analysis grid cells were defined as "zones" and zonal means of average patch size were calculated based on the 30 m resolution cells that fell in each zone. The actual measure used in the analysis is 1 minus the ratio of average patch size to the maximum possible patch size. The broad land cover classes (forest, shrub, and grass) are as defined in EDG except that grass patches do not include herbaceous wetlands.	Patch-based measure of fragmentation, 2002: Data made available on CD-ROM in ASCII and SAS format, prepared by USDA Forest Service, Research Triangle Park, NC: Forestry Sciences Lab, Forest Health Monitoring (SRS-4803), 2002. Fragmentation databases will be available at http://www.srs.fs.usda.gov/4803/landscapes/index.html. See also Riitters (2004) and Küchler (1993).
EXT	Exotic breeding birds. Proportion of total exotic individuals to total individuals (exotic + native) for each BBS route averaged over the years the route was run between 1990 – 1998, then kriged to analysis grid cell centroids.	North American Breeding Bird Survey (BBS), USGS Patuxent Wildlife Research Center, Laurel, MD. 2001. http://www.pwrc.usgs.gov/bbs/retrieval/menu.cfm.
MOR	Mortality of growing stock on timberlands in 1000 cu. ft./acre/yr standardized to volume of growing stock on timberlands in 1000 cu. ft./acre/yr by county, then kriged to analysis grid cell centroids.	National RPA Forest Data Base, 1997: Data made available in ASCII file format, prepared by USDA Forest Service, Asheville, NC: Forest Inventory and Monitoring (SRS-4801), 1999. USDA Forest Service. Forest Inventory and Analysis (FIA). 1997 National RPA Forest Data Base (Eastwide /Westwide format). http://srs fia2.fs.fed.us/html/tables.htm. See also Hansen and others (1992) and Woudenberg and Farrenkopf (1995).

| GRO | Measure of actual productivity on timberlands (growth in cu. ft./acre/yr) divided by potential productivity on timberlands. Potential productivity is also in cu. ft./acre/yr and is calculated based on site productivity class. The actual measure used in the analysis is 1 minus this proportion. This data is recorded by county and was kriged to analysis grid cell centroids. | National RPA Forest Data Base, 1997: Data made available in ASCII file format, prepared by USDA Forest Service, Asheville, NC: Forest Inventory and Monitoring (SRS-4801), 1999.

USDA Forest Service. Forest Inventory and Analysis (FIA). 1997 National RPA Forest Data Base (Eastwide /Westwide format). http://srs fia2.fs.fed.us/html/tables.htm.

See also Hansen and others (1992) and Woudenberg and Farrenkopf (1995). |

| STR | The mean yearly streamflows (in cfs) in the 1990's and the 30-year period 1960 to 1989 were standardized to drainage areas in sq. mi. with 6826 and 1240 sample points, respectively. Both of these values were kriged to analysis grid cell centroids. Then, the 30-year averages were divided into the streamflows from the 1990s. The actual measure used in the analysis is 1 minus this proportion. | USGS daily and peak values data compiled on CD-ROM by Hydrosphere Data Products, Inc. Boulder, CO. 1999. http://www.hydrosphere. com/hdp/.

USGS Fact Sheet FS-027-98. National Water Information System (NWIS). http://pubs.usgs. gov/fs/FS-027-98/.

See also Yorke and Williams (1991). |

| NTG | Total nitrogen measured as mg/L in surface waters. Kriged to analysis grid cell centroids from 34,131 sample point locations. | STORET (mainframe) Water Quality File (now STORET Legacy Data), 1998: Nutrient parameter files obtained from USEPA anonymous ftp site, prepared by staff of the USEPA, Washington, DC: USEPA Data Storage and Retrieval System (STORET), 1999.

USEPA, Office of Water, STORET Legacy Data Center (USGS data removed), 1999. http:// www.epa.gov/storpubl/legacy/gateway.htm.

USEPA, STORET, About STORET, 2002. http://www.epa.gov/STORET/about.html.

USGS, National Water Information System (NWISWeb), Water-Quality Data for the Nation, 1999. http://waterdata.usgs.gov/nwis/qw.

USGS Fact Sheet FS-027-98. National Water Information System (NWIS). http://pubs.usgs. gov/fs/FS-027-98/.

See also Yorke and Williams (1991). |

| PHO | Total phosphorus measured as mg/L in surface waters. Kriged to analysis grid cell centroids from 45,283 sample point locations. | STORET (mainframe) Water Quality File (now STORET Legacy Data), 1998: Nutrient parameter files obtained from USEPA anony mous ftp site, prepared by staff of the USEPA, Washington, DC: USEPA Data Storage and Retrieval System (STORET), 1999. |

		USEPA, Office of Water, STORET Legacy Data Center (USGS data removed), 1999. http://www.epa.gov/storpubl/legacy/gateway.htm.

USEPA, STORET, About STORET, 2002. http://www.epa.gov/STORET/about.html.

USGS, National Water Information System (NWISWeb), Water-Quality Data for the Nation, 1999. http://waterdata.usgs.gov/nwis/qw.

USGS Fact Sheet FS-027-98. National Water Information System (NWIS). http://pubs.usgs.gov/fs/FS-027-98/.

See also Yorke and Williams (1991). |
| PHL | Lab pH. Calculated using a 2500 m grid of hydrogen ion concentrations in precipitation collected at field locations and measured in the lab. In a GIS procedure, the analysis grid cells were defined as "zones" and zonal means of hydrogen ion concentrations were calculated based on the 2500 m resolution cells that fell in each zone. The hydrogen ion concentrations were then converted to pH. The actual measure used in the analysis was the observed average pH subtracted from the value 7 (all observations were less than 7). | National Atmospheric Deposition Program (NADP) Maps, 1998: ARC/INFO grids of lab pH obtained from NADP anonymous ftp site, prepared by NADP Program Office, Champaign, IL: Illinois State Water Survey. 2000.

National Atmospheric Deposition Program (NRSP-3) National Trends Network. 1998. NADP Program Office, Illinois State Water Survey, 2204 Griffith Dr., Champaign, IL 61820. http://nadp.sws.uiuc.edu/. |
| TRI | Total toxic chemical releases to the environment for each county (air, water, and land). Measured in pounds per acre. These data were kriged to analysis grid cell centroids. | USEPA, Toxics Release Inventory (TRI), EZ Query, 1997. http://www.epa.gov/enviro/html/tris/ez.html.

USEPA, Toxics Release Inventory (TRI) Program, What is the Toxics Release Inventory (TRI) Program, 2002. http://www.epa.gov/tri/whatis.htm. |

Human Activity Variables:

FED	Federal land areas as a proportion of total area by analysis grid cell. In a GIS procedure, a geographic intersection of a polygon coverage of federal land areas and a polygon coverage of the analysis grid enabled the calculation of this proportion. The data included only federal areas greater than 640 acres. It also did not include "linear" areas such as federally administered parkways.	USGS, Federal Lands and Indian Reservations of the United States, 2003. http://nationalatlas.gov/atlasftp.html.

PAD	Protected areas of the U.S. as a proportion of total area by analysis grid cell. In a GIS procedure, a geographic intersection of a polygon coverage of protected areas and a polygon coverage of the analysis grid enabled the calculation of this proportion. Protected areas are defined as parcels with a Gap Analysis Program (GAP) code of 1 or 2. The actual measure used in the analysis is 1 minus this proportion.	CBI/WWF Protected Areas Database (PAD), Second Edition. 2001. http://www.consbio. org/cbi/applied_research/pad_2005/pad2005. htm. See also DellaSala and others (2001).
RNG	Proportion of counties in rangeland. A land cover/use category on which the climax or potential plant cover is composed principally of native grasses, grasslike plants, forbs or shrubs suitable for grazing and browsing, and introduced forage species that are managed like rangeland. This would include areas where introduced hardy and persistent grasses, such as crested wheatgrass, are planted and such practices as deferred grazing, burning, chaining, and rotational grazing are used, with little or no chemicals or fertilizer being applied. Grasslands, savannas, many wetlands, some deserts, and tundra are considered to be rangeland. Certain communities of low forbs and shrubs, such as mesquite, chaparral, mountain shrub, and pinyon-juniper, are also considered as rangeland. These data were kriged to analysis grid cell centroids.	Summary Report, 1997 National Resources Inventory (NRI). See Appendix 3, Glossary of Selected Terms, revised December 2000.
CRO	Proportion of counties in crops. A land cover/ use category that includes areas used for the production of adapted crops for harvest. Cropland includes cultivated and noncultivated lands. Cultivated cropland includes row crops, close-grown crops, and other cultivated cropland such as hayland or pastureland that is in a rotation with row or close-grown crops. Noncultivated cropland includes permanent hayland and horticultural cropland. These data were kriged to analysis grid cell centroids.	Same as RNG.
FOR	Proportion of counties in forest land. A land cover/use category that is at least 10 percent stocked by single-stemmed woody species of any size that will be at least 4 meters tall at maturity. Land bearing evidence of natural regeneration of tree cover (cut over forest or abandoned farmland) and not currently developed for nonforest use is also included. Ten percent stocking, when viewed from a	Same as RNG.

vertical direction, equates to an areal canopy cover of leaves and branches of 25 percent or greater. The minimum area for classification as forest land is 1 acre, and the area must be at least 100 feet wide. These data were kriged to analysis grid cell centroids.

DEV	Proportion of counties in developed land. A land cover/use category that includes "large" (>10 acres) and "small" (.25-10 acres) urban and built-up areas. These include residential, industrial, commercial, and institutional land; construction sites; public administrative sites; railroad yards; cemeteries; airports; golf courses; sanitary landfills; sewage treatment plants; water control structures and spillways; other land used for such purposes; small parks within urban and built-up areas; and highways, railroads, and other transportation facilities if they are surrounded by urban areas. Also included are tracts of less than 10 acres that do not meet the above definition but are completely surrounded by urban and built-up land. These data were kriged to analysis grid centroids.	Same as RNG.
PAS	Proportion of counties in pastureland. A land cover/use category of land managed primarily for the production of introduced forage plants for livestock grazing. Pastureland may consist of a single species in a pure stand, a grass mixture, or a grass-legume mixture. Management usually consists of cultural treatments: fertilization, weed control, reseeding or renovation, and control of grazing. For the NRI, includes land that has a vegetative cover of grasses, legumes, and/or forbs, regardless of whether or not it is being grazed by livestock. These data were kriged to analysis grid cell centroids.	Same as RNG.
CRP	Proportion of counties in the Conservation Reserve Program (CRP), a federal program established under the Food Security Act of 1985 to assist private landowners to convert highly erodible cropland to vegetative cover for 10 years. These data were kriged to analysis grid centroids.	Same as RNG.

| POP | Human population density within each county. These data were kriged to analysis grid cell centroids. | Census 2000 Summary File 1 United States. Prepared by the U.S. Census Bureau, 2001. |

Stratification:

| DIV | A categorical variable that stratifies the coterminous U.S. into 3 ecoregional classifications based on "divisional" boundaries from Bailey's Ecoregions of the United States. Each analysis grid cell was assigned to an ecoregion category with a GIS procedure (using a geographic intersection of polygon coverages). | Bailey, R. G. 1995. Description of the ecoregions of the United States, 2nd ed. Revised and expanded (1st ed. 1980). Misc. Publ. No. 1391 (rev.), USDA Forest Service, Washington, DC. 108p. with separate map. |

Climate and Topographic Variables:

| TMP | Mean annual temperature. In a GIS Procedure, analysis grid cells were defined as zones and zonal means of gridded mean annual temperature (30-year normals, 1961-1990) were calculated. Measured in $F°$. 10. Original data was on a 4 km grid such that the zonal mean was based on ~25 observations. | Oregon State University, Spatial Climate Analysis Service (SCAS) and Oregon Climate Service (OCS), PRISM digital climate data, 1996. http://www.ocs.orst.edu/prism/.

Oregon State University, Spatial Climate Analysis Service (SCAS) and Oregon Climate Service (OCS), Climate Mapping with PRISM, Reports and Papers. 1993-1998. http://www.ocs.orst.edu/prism/docs/index.phtml. |

| TMS | Spatial variation in temperature. In a GIS procedure, analysis grid cells were defined as zones and zonal standard deviations of gridded mean annual temperature (30-year normals, 1961-1990) were calculated. Original data was on a 4 km grid such that the zonal mean was based on ~25 observations. | Oregon State University, Spatial Climate Analysis Service (SCAS) and Oregon Climate Service (OCS), PRISM digital climate data, 1996. http://www.ocs.orst.edu/prism/.

Oregon State University, Spatial Climate Analysis Service (SCAS) and Oregon Climate Service (OCS), Climate Mapping with PRISM, Reports and Papers. 1993-1998. http://www.ocs.orst.edu/prism/docs/index.phtml. |

| SST | Seasonal variation in temperature. In a GIS procedure, analysis grid cells were defined as zones and zonal means of gridded mean monthly temperatures (30-year normals, 1961-1990) were calculated. The standard deviation across mean monthly temperatures then was used as a measure of seasonal variation in temperature. Original data was on a 4 km grid such that the zonal mean was based on ~25 observations. | Oregon State University, Spatial Climate Analysis Service (SCAS) and Oregon Climate Service (OCS), PRISM digital climate data, 1996. http://www.ocs.orst.edu/prism/.

Oregon State University, Spatial Climate Analysis Service (SCAS) and Oregon Climate Service (OCS), Climate Mapping with PRISM, Reports and Papers. 1993-1998. http://www.ocs.orst.edu/prism/docs/index.phtml. |

AVT	Temporal variation in temperature. VEMAP data (historical data, 1895 to 1993) on a 0.5°X 0.5° degree grid of latitude and longitude were used to calculate the standard deviation of 99 years of mean annual temperature observations at each of 3261 lat/lon locations, then kriged to analysis grid cell centroids.	National Center for Atmospheric Research (NCAR), Ecosystem Dynamics and the Atmosphere Section, VEMAP 2 Transient Climate Datasets (TCLIMATE), Monthly Files, Historical Climate (1895-1993). 1998. http://www.cgd.ucar.edu:80/vemap/ve298.html. See also Kittel and others (1997).
PRC	Mean annual precipitation. Calculated using same method as for TMP. Measured in mm. Original data was on a 4 km grid such that the zonal mean was based on ~25 observations.	Oregon State University, Spatial Climate Analysis Service (SCAS) and Oregon Climate Service (OCS), PRISM digital climate data, 1996. http://www.ocs.orst.edu/prism/. Oregon State University, Spatial Climate Analysis Service (SCAS) and Oregon Climate Service (OCS), Climate Mapping with PRISM, Reports and Papers. 1993-1998. http://www.ocs.orst.edu/prism/docs/index.phtml.
PRS	Spatial variation in precipitation. Calculated using same method as for TMS. Original data was on a 4 km grid such that the zonal mean was based on ~25 observations.	Oregon State University, Spatial Climate Analysis Service (SCAS) and Oregon Climate Service (OCS), PRISM digital climate data, 1996. http://www.ocs.orst.edu/prism/. Oregon State University, Spatial Climate Analysis Service (SCAS) and Oregon Climate Service (OCS), Climate Mapping with PRISM, Reports and Papers. 1993-1998. http://www.ocs.orst.edu/prism/docs/index.phtml.
SSP	Seasonal variation in precipitation. Calculated using same method as for SST. Original data was on a 4 km grid such that the zonal mean was based on ~25 observations.	Oregon State University, Spatial Climate Analysis Service (SCAS) and Oregon Climate Service (OCS), PRISM digital climate data, 1996. http://www.ocs.orst.edu/prism/. Oregon State University, Spatial Climate Analysis Service (SCAS) and Oregon Climate Service (OCS), Climate Mapping with PRISM, Reports and Papers. 1993-1998. http://www.ocs.orst.edu/prism/docs/index.phtml.
AVP	Temporal variation in precipitation. Calculated using same method as for AVT.	National Center for Atmospheric Research (NCAR), Ecosystem Dynamics and the Atmosphere Section, VEMAP 2 Transient Climate Datasets (TCLIMATE), Monthly Files, Historical Climate (1895-1993). 1998. http://www.cgd.ucar.edu:80/vemap/ve298.html. See also Kittel and others (1997).

VEG	Total vegetation carbon (potential – no land use effects). Thirty-year annual average (1961-1990) gC/m^2 at 3168 lat/lon locations representing the center of a 0.5°X 0.5° grid, then kriged to analysis grid cell centroids.	National Center for Atmospheric Research (NCAR), Ecosystem Dynamics and the Atmosphere Section, VEMAP2 Transient Dynamics Data, distributed by the University of New Hampshire, EOS-WEBSTER Earth Science Information Partner (ESIP), dataset TResults-CGCM1-Increasing CO2. 2000. http://eos-webster.sr.unh.edu/data_guides/vemap_trans_dg.jsp.
		See also Schimel and others (2000).
DEM	Mean elevation. In a GIS procedure, analysis grid cells were defined as zones and zonal means of gridded elevation data were calculated. Measured in meters.	Oregon State University, Oregon Climate Service FTP Archive, Conterminous U.S. 2.5-minute Digital Elevation Model (DEM), 1995. ftp://www.ocs.orst.edu/pub/maps/Other/U.S./.
		See also Barnes (1964)
DMS	Elevation variance. In a GIS procedure, analysis grid cells were defined as zones and zonal standard deviations of gridded elevation data were calculated.	Oregon State University, Oregon Climate Service FTP Archive, Conterminous U.S. 2.5-minute Digital Elevation Model (DEM), 1995. ftp://www.ocs.orst.edu/pub/maps/Other/U.S./.
		See also Barnes (1964).

Appendix B: Mapped Current and Projected Explanatory Variables

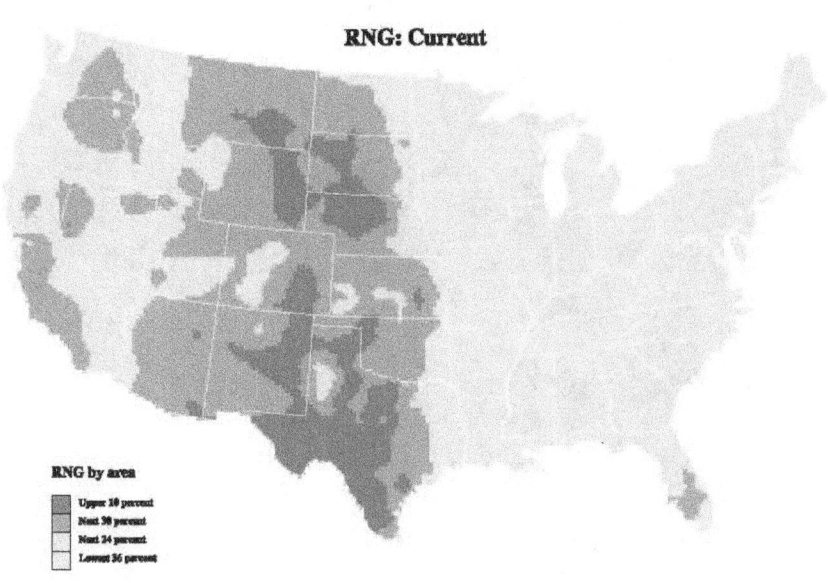

RNG: Current

RNG by area
- Upper 10 percent
- Next 30 percent
- Next 24 percent
- Lowest 36 percent

Figure 13. (a) Current Conditions and (b) Projections to 2025 for RNG. Classes depicted in the projection map (b) have maintained the class cutpoints used to define the current condition (a).

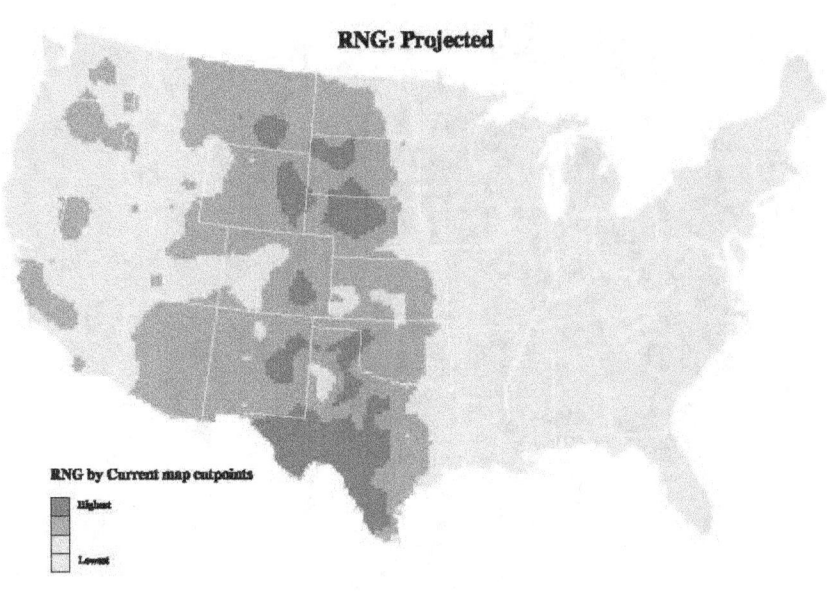

RNG: Projected

RNG by Current map cutpoints
- Highest
- Lowest

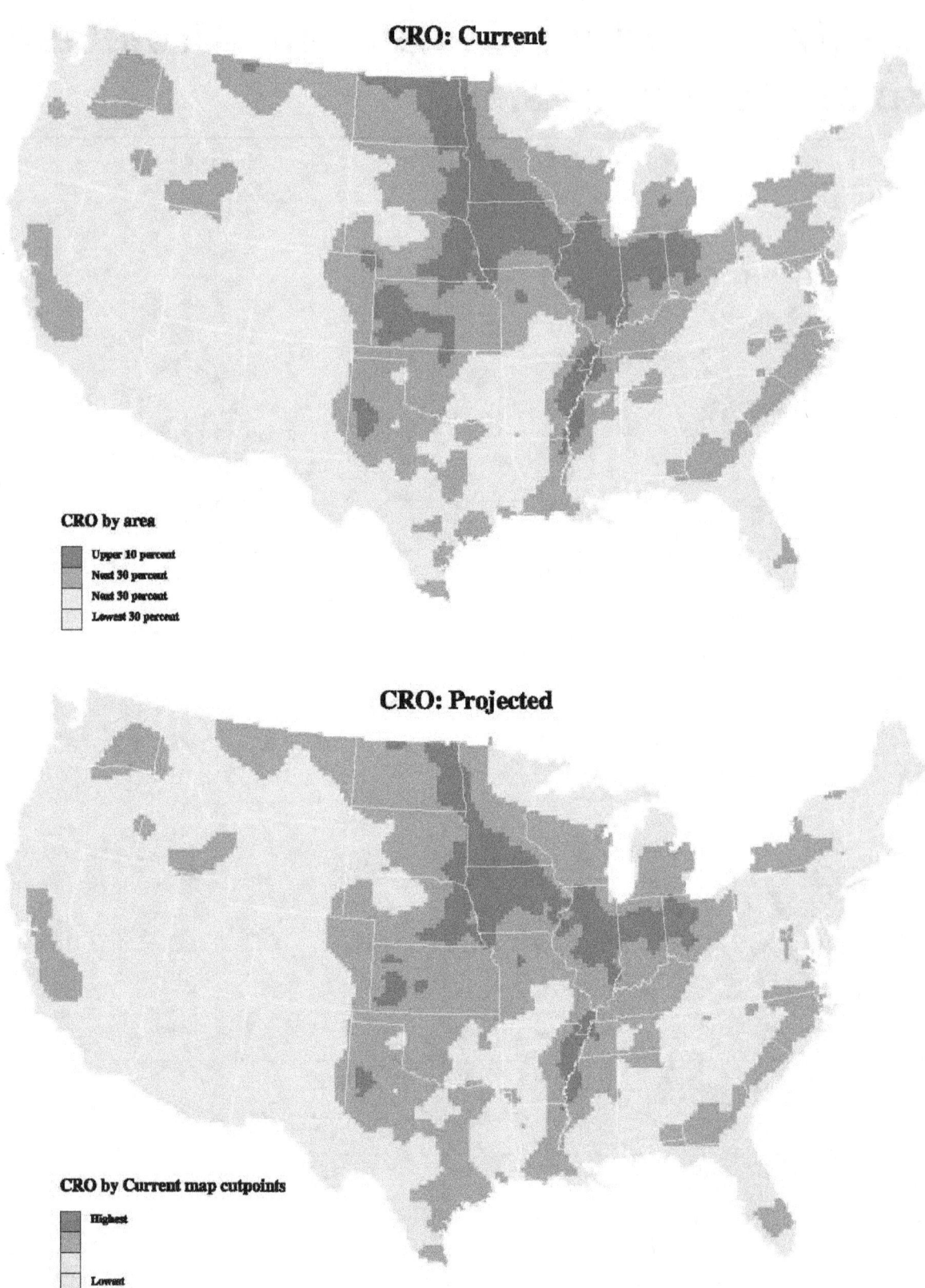

Figure 14. (a) Current Conditions and (b) Projections to 2025 for CRO. Classes depicted in the projection map (b) have maintained the class cutpoints used to define the current condition (a).

USDA Forest Service RMRS-GTR-166. 2006.

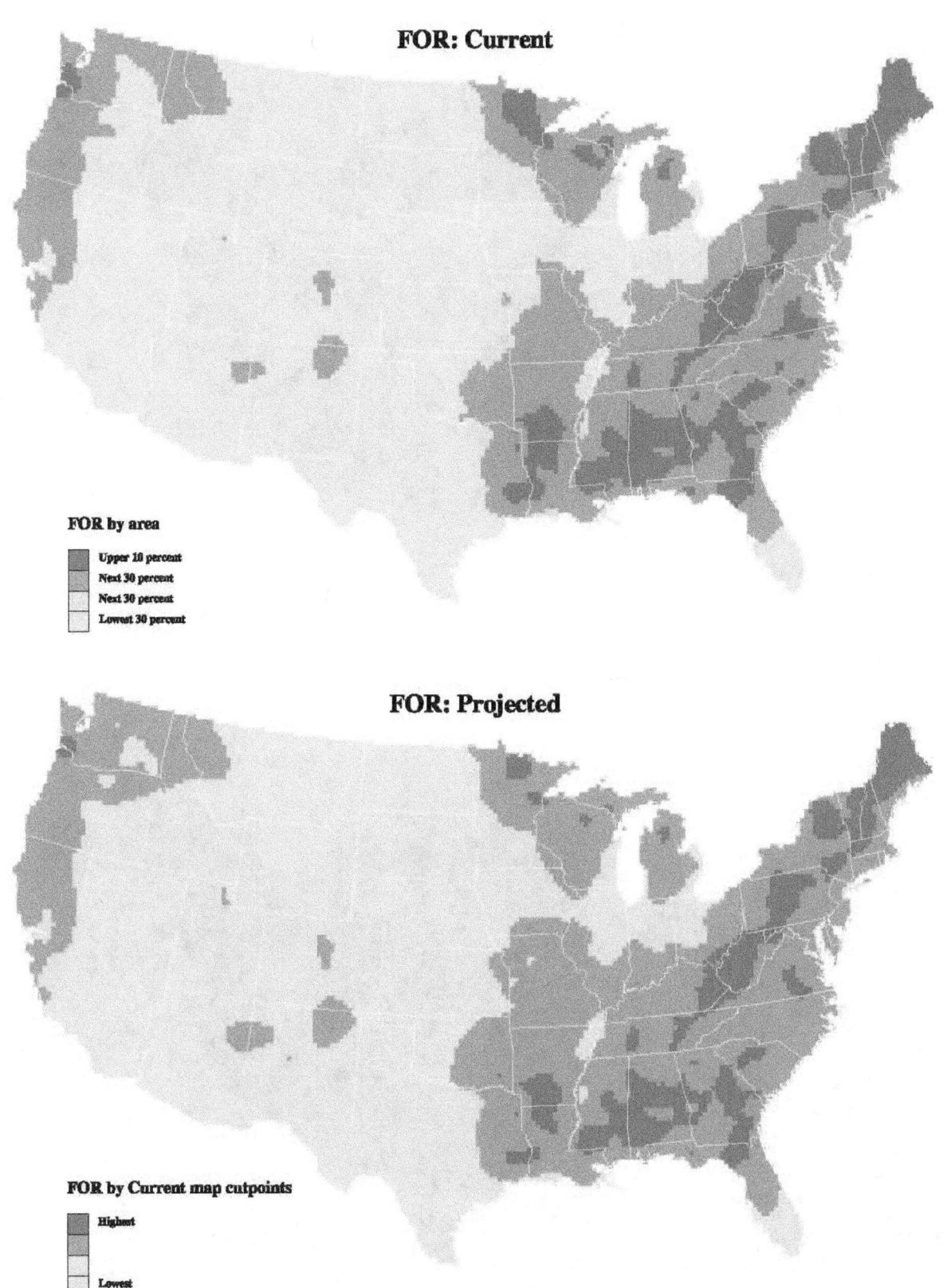

Figure 15. (a) Current Conditions and (b) Projections to 2025 for FOR. Classes depicted in the projection map (b) have maintained the class cutpoints used to define the current condition (a).

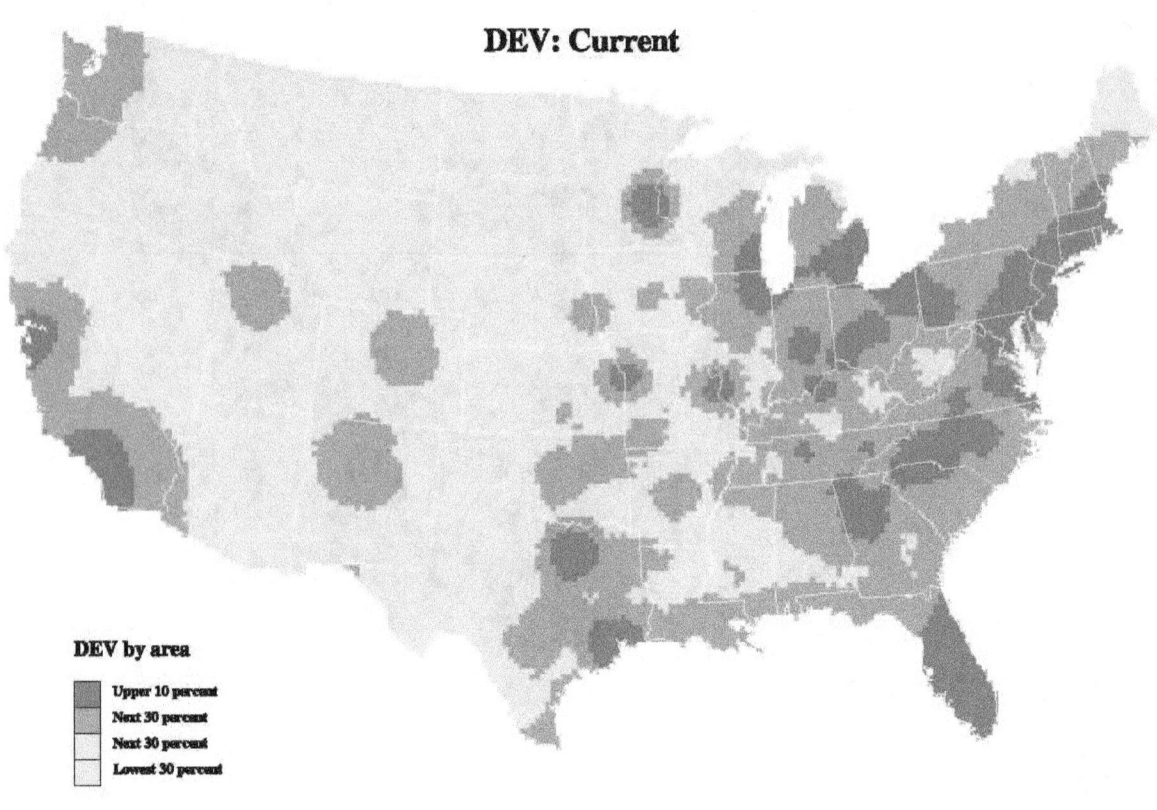

DEV: Current

DEV by area

- Upper 10 percent
- Next 30 percent
- Next 30 percent
- Lowest 30 percent

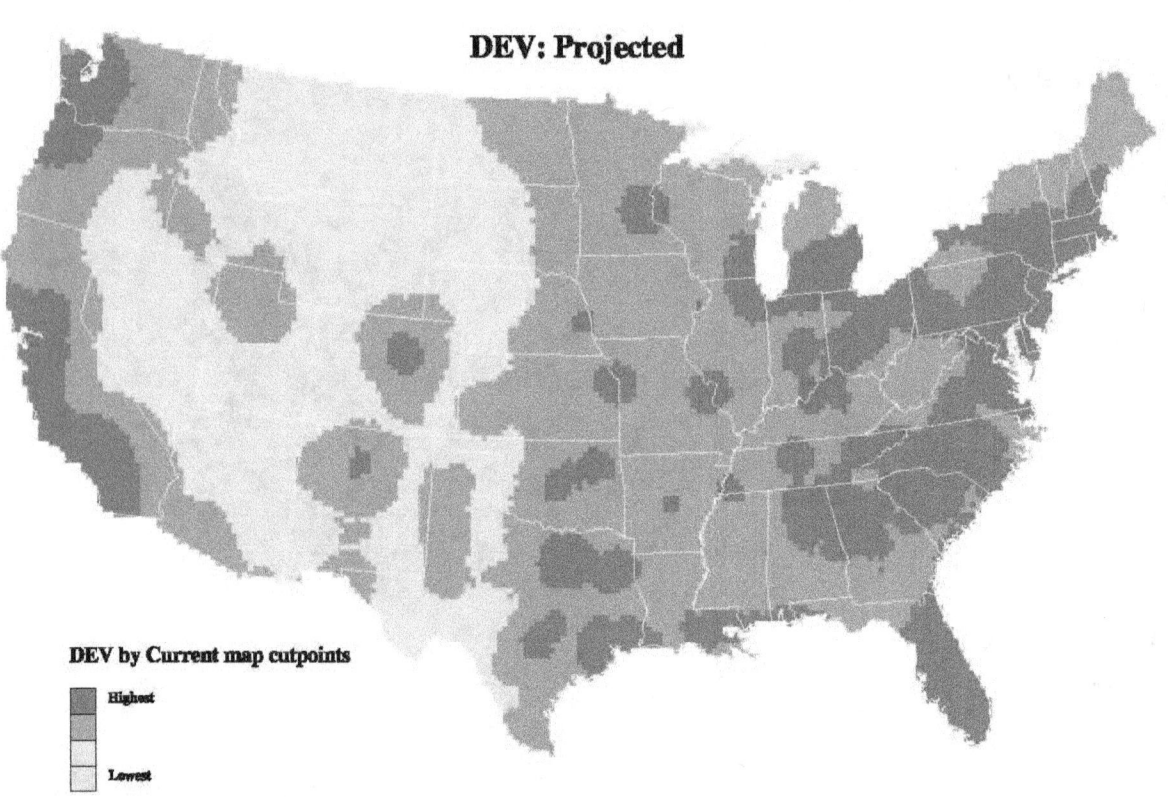

DEV: Projected

DEV by Current map cutpoints

- Highest
- Lowest

Figure 16. (a) Current Conditions and (b) Projections to 2025 for DEV. Classes depicted in the projection map (b) have maintained the class cutpoints used to define the current condition (a).

PAS: Current

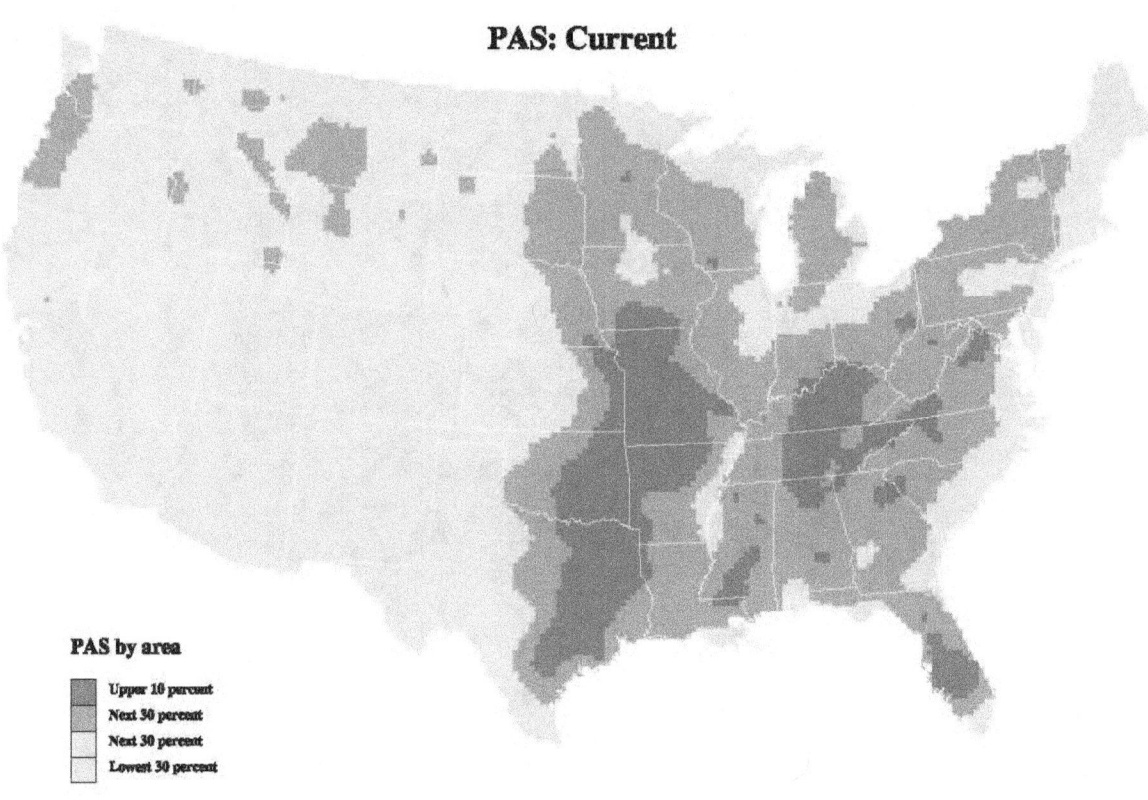

PAS by area

- Upper 10 percent
- Next 30 percent
- Next 30 percent
- Lowest 30 percent

PAS: Projected

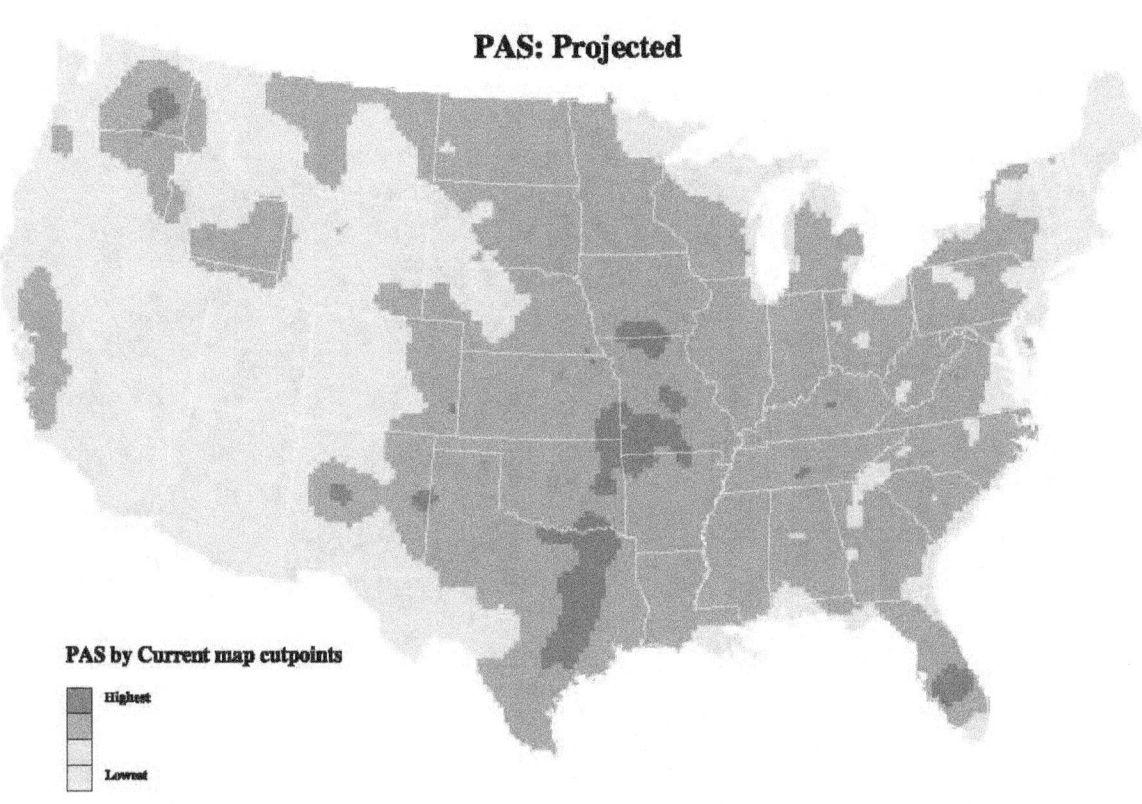

PAS by Current map cutpoints

- Highest
- Lowest

Figure 17. (a) Current Conditions and (b) Projections to 2025 for PAS. Classes depicted in the projection map (b) have maintained the class cutpoints used to define the current condition (a).

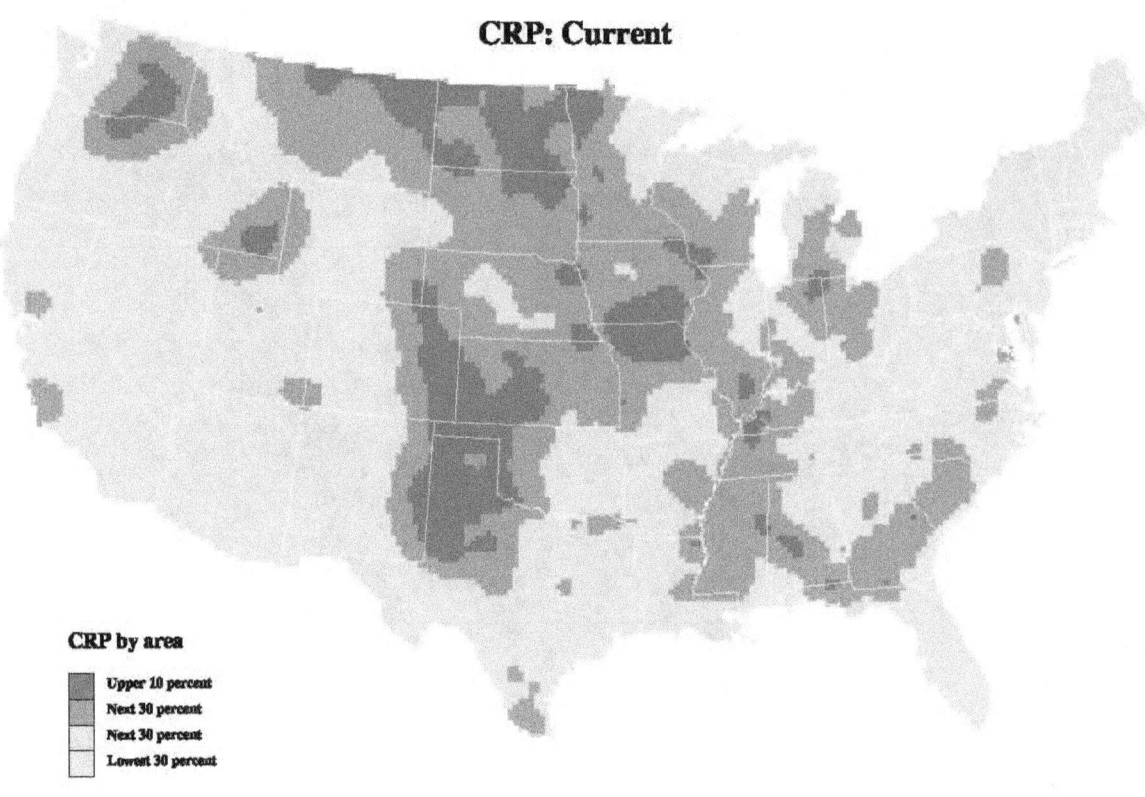

CRP: Current

CRP by area

Upper 10 percent
Next 30 percent
Next 30 percent
Lowest 30 percent

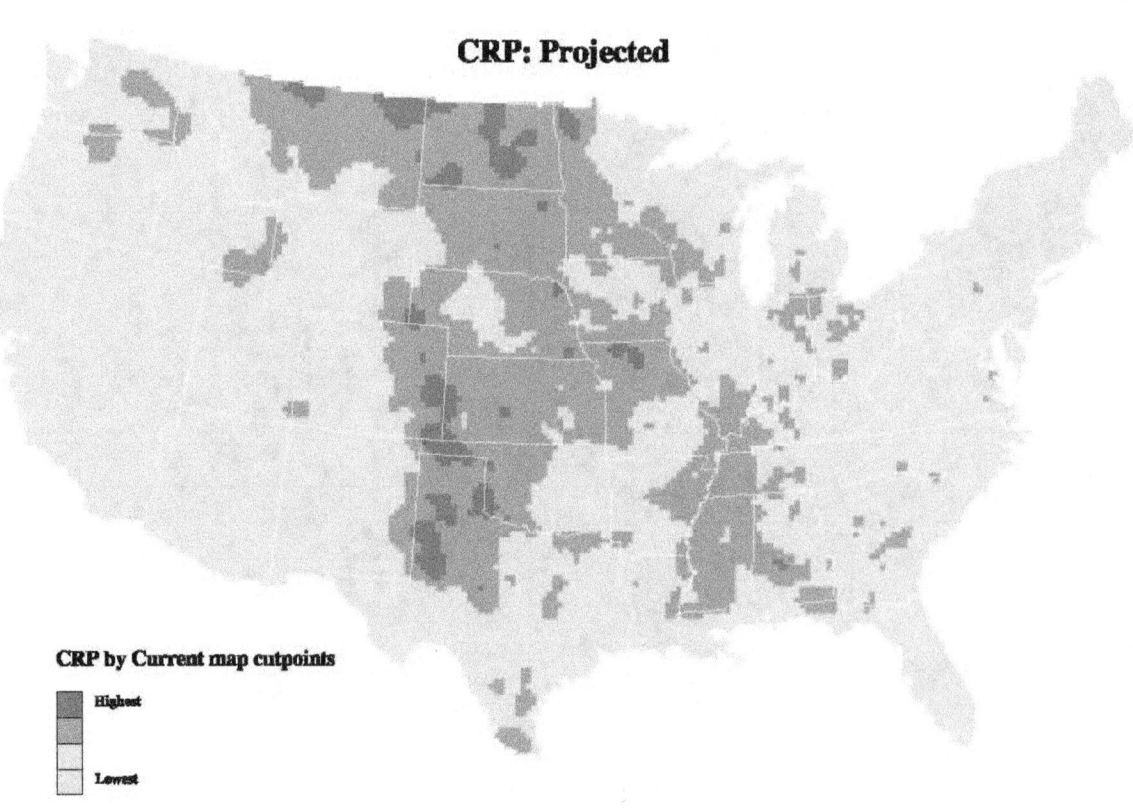

CRP: Projected

CRP by Current map cutpoints

Highest

Lowest

Figure 18. (a) Current Conditions and (b) Projections to 2025 for CRP. Classes depicted in the projection map (b) have maintained the class cutpoints used to define the current condition (a).

POP: Current

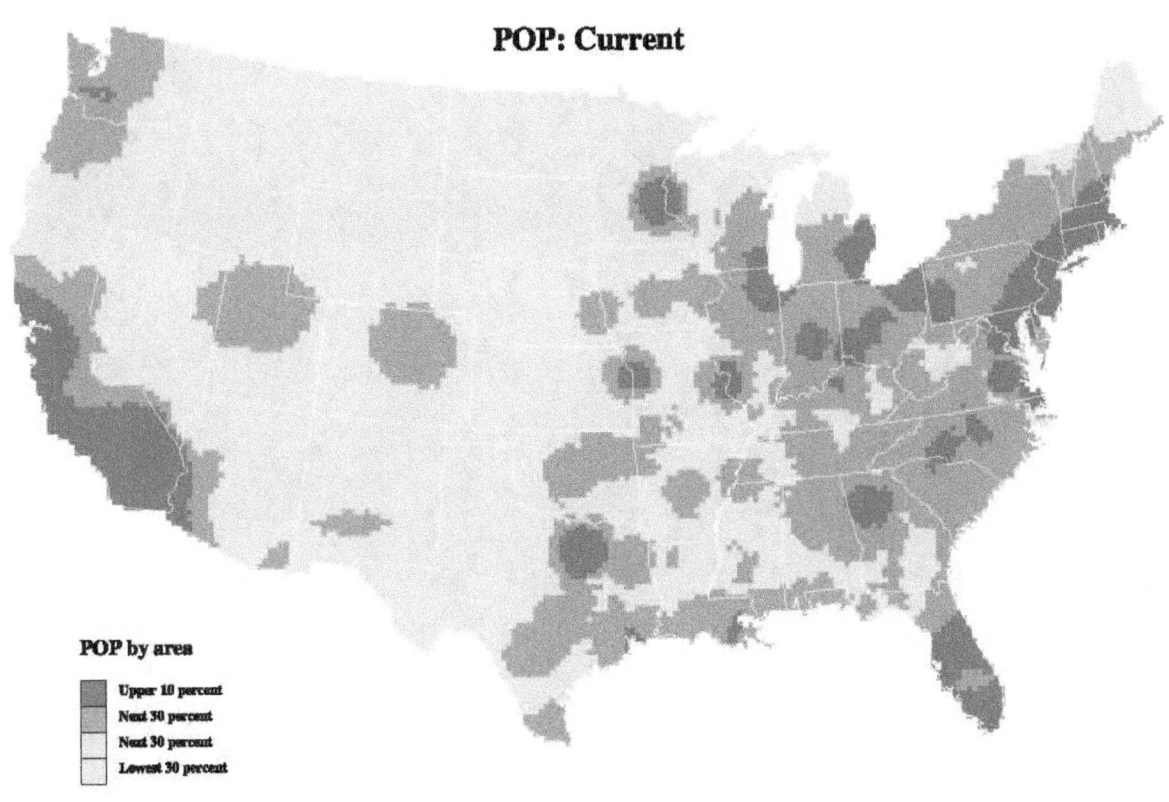

POP by area

- Upper 10 percent
- Next 30 percent
- Next 30 percent
- Lowest 30 percent

POP: Projected

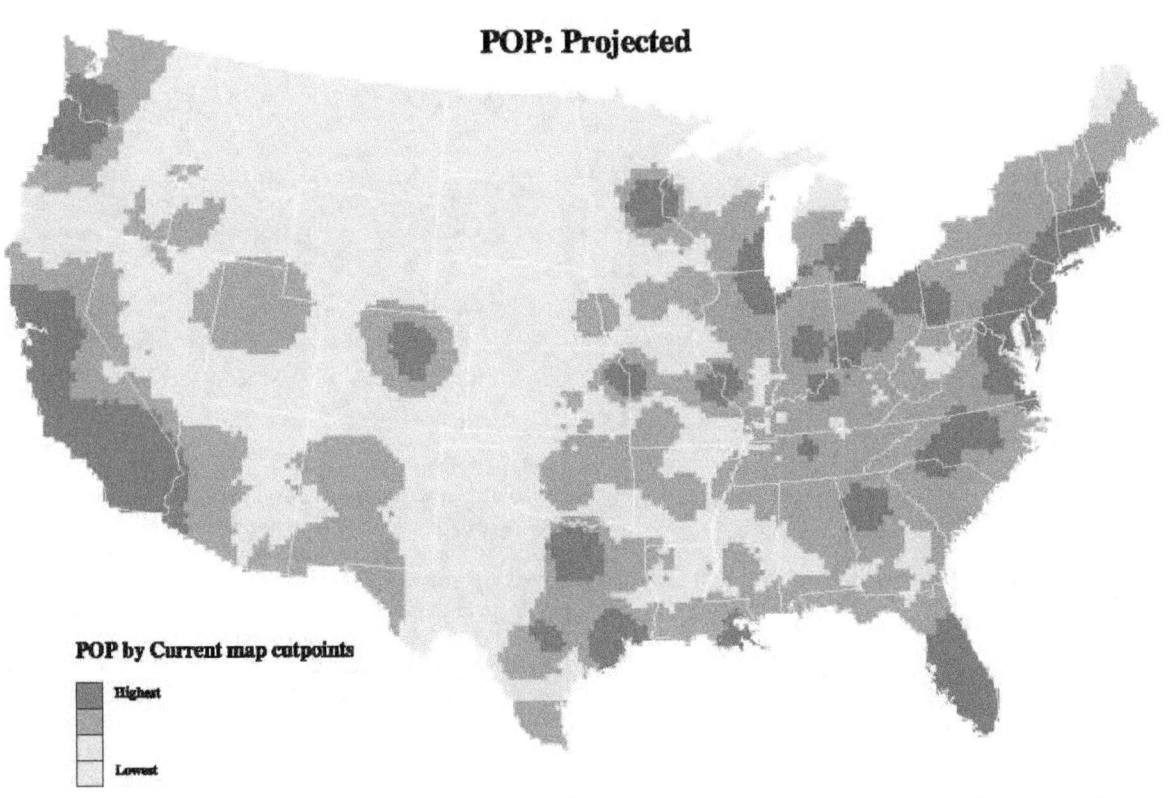

POP by Current map cutpoints

- Highest
- Lowest

Figure 19. (a) Current Conditions and (b) Projections to 2025 for POP. Classes depicted in the projection map (b) have maintained the class cutpoints used to define the current condition (a).